BEGIN BOLDLY

How Women Can Reimagine Risk, Embrace Uncertainty, and Launch a Brilliant Career

....

CHRISTIE HUNTER ARSCOTT

BK

Berrett–Koehler Publishers, Inc.

Berrett-Koehler Publishers, Inc.
1333 Broadway, Suite 1000
Oakland, CA 94612–1921
Tel: (510) 817–2277
Fax: (510) 817–2278
www.bkconnection.com

ORDERING INFORMATION

Quantity sales. Special discounts are available on quantity purchases by corporations, associations, and others. For details, contact the "Special Sales Department" at the Berrett-Koehler address above.

Individual sales. Berrett-Koehler publications are available through most bookstores. They can also be ordered directly from Berrett-Koehler: Tel: (800) 929–2929; Fax: (802) 864–7626; www.bkconnection.com.

Orders for college textbook / course adoption use. Please contact Berrett-Koehler: Tel: (800) 929–2929; Fax: (802) 864–7626.

Distributed to the U.S. trade and internationally by Penguin Random House Publisher Services.

Berrett-Koehler and the BK logo are registered trademarks of Berrett-Koehler Publishers, Inc.

Printed in the United States of America

Berrett-Koehler books are printed on long-lasting acid-free paper. When it is available, we choose paper that has been manufactured by environmentally responsible processes. These may include using trees grown in sustainable forests, incorporating recycled paper, minimizing chlorine in bleaching, or recycling the energy produced at the paper mill.

Library of Congress Cataloging-in-Publication Data

Names: Hunter Arscott, Christie, author.
Title: Begin Boldly : How Women Can Reimagine Risk, Embrace Uncertainty, and Launch a Brilliant Career / Christie Hunter Arscott.
Description: First Edition. | Oakland, CA : Berrett-Koehler Publishers, [2022] | Includes bibliographical references and index.
Identifiers: LCCN 2021060253 (print) | LCCN 2021060254 (ebook) | ISBN 9781523001071 (paperback) | ISBN 9781523001088 (pdf) | ISBN 9781523001095 (epub)
Subjects: LCSH: Women college graduates—Employment. | Sex discrimination in employment. | Women—Vocational guidance. | Career development. | Experience.
Classification: LCC HD6053.5 .A73 2022 (print) | LCC HD6053.5 (ebook) | DDC 650.14082—dc23/eng/20220211
LC record available at https://lccn.loc.gov/2021060253
LC ebook record available at https://lccn.loc.gov/2021060254

First Edition
28 27 26 25 24 23 22   10 9 8 7 6 5 4 3 2

Cover and text designer: Debbie Berne
Author photographs: Meredith Andrews

For Janet and Scott—

To the ones who nurtured the bold spirit within me.
It is my gift to continue to ignite that flame in others.

Contents

Foreword by Betsy Myers

It is an honor to welcome Christie Hunter Arscott to the top ranks of leadership authors with her significant book, a must read for early career women. Over the years of knowing Christie, she has inspired me with her fresh perspectives about women and leadership. I count Christie among my cherished colleagues and friends.

Christie is the perfect person to write this book, *Begin Boldly*. This labor of love comes from her head—her personal experiences and lessons learned in her own early-stage career—and from her heart, her desire to support the next generation of young women. She brings a wealth of wisdom and knowledge as a leadership expert, coach, and public speaker. True to her advice, she has consistently embraced her own uncertainty, taking bold moves that have informed her career, including writing this book!

There are two pieces of debilitating thinking that hold women back: The first is waiting to be noticed or appreciated. The other is not taking a risk to apply for a new job or opportunity, believing that they do not have enough experience or skill sets. Christie turns this thinking on its head. She challenges young women to do the opposite and treat their career like an investment portfolio with early deposits of bold moves, courageous actions, and informed risk. I could not agree more!

Taking risks took me to the White House as President Clinton's senior adviser on women's issues, executive director of the Center for Public Leadership at Harvard's Kennedy School of Government, chief operating officer of President Obama's 2007–08 presidential campaign, and a book deal with Atria books at Simon & Schuster.

Each was a stretch assignment and out of my comfort zone. I surrounded myself with talented, experienced staff that had my back and I asked for help. One of the key concepts of Christie's book that completely resonates—*when we take a bold move or courageous action, trust in our ability to figure it out!*

In her undeniably significant book, Christie gives the most important advice for early-stage women leaders: *build a friendship with risk and uncertainty*. It is the key differentiator between an average career and a brilliant career.

Even better—she shows you how.

This gem of a book is a valuable resource for every woman, at every stage, who has big dreams and aspirations. I can't wait for you to meet Christie through the pages of this book!

Betsy Myers is author of *Take The Lead* and a former senior adviser on women's issues to President Barack Obama and President Bill Clinton.

Preface: "Woman Up!"

"Woman up!" These words appeared on my computer screen as my Microsoft Office messenger pinged. To my surprise, they were sent from a senior-level partner at my organization who was on the same team call as I was. With my best interests at heart, this partner was calling me out for sitting quietly during the session with other consultants and not advocating for myself or the work I had done, not asking questions, and not using my voice. Instead of saying "Man up," she was rephrasing it in the hope that I would "Woman up" and be bolder and braver in these discussions. To her dismay, I sat silently while others dominated the conversation and failed to attribute my contributions and ideas to me.

Not long before this call, at the age of twenty-five, I entered the world of consulting in corporate America, jumping into the Manhattan landscape of demanding clients, deadlines, and pressures. When I transitioned from university to a professional career, there was no shortage of resources designed to help me make that leap. How to craft my résumé. How to nail an interview. How to make myself stand out in a competitive job market. However, once I was in the workforce, I discovered that there was a notable lack of similar support to help me achieve success in that all-important first role and the early career years that followed. It felt as if I had suddenly been thrown into uncharted waters and was now floating in an ocean of uncertainty without a life jacket, barely keeping my head above the surface. With a pervasive fear of failure and fear of the unknown, I clung to what I could control, or thought I could control, and too often played it safe rather than playing it smart. While feeling inexperienced and grappling with self-doubt, I favored the comfort of the known over the uncertainty of risk.

If you have ever felt this way, you are not alone. One of the biggest challenges that women face in their careers is navigating the transitions during their first ten years, including the shift from university to first career role. When you're in a new environment and confronting unknowns, it's tempting to retreat to a place that seems safe and seek out certainty in order to feel a sense of control. However, this is the same as clinging to the shore instead of learning how to swim.

Fast-forward to where I am today: I've built a career based on taking risks and riding the waves, through the ebbs and flows of a dynamic profession focused on empowering and equipping women to build bold and brilliant careers and lives. I've had successes and highs, speaking in front of thousands, winning international awards, being published, running a six-figure business, and most important, making a meaningful and lasting impact on the individuals and organizations I work with. I've also endured some notable lows, including rejections, contracts that didn't materialize, proposals turned down, opportunities lost, and risks gone wrong. What has fueled my growth has been the view that each risk that I don't take may be the opposing force against building a career and life I love. The question for me isn't just "What happens if I risk?" It's also "What happens if I don't?" I desired to learn how to swim, dive deep, and explore the endless possibilities of my career rather than cling to the safety of the shore. And I am glad I started to do this earlier rather than later, giving me more time to maximize my career journey.

What helped catalyze my shift from fearing risk to seeking risk? I've been in the fortunate position to learn from the women who came before me. The last fifteen years of researching and working with professional women have revealed one often-overlooked skill that is formative in the early years: knowing *how to take risks*. The surprising truth: Risks are a good thing, provided that they are taken thoughtfully and strategically. My research has highlighted that risk-taking is enlightening and empowering and is the antidote for self-doubt. By taking a chance on themselves, women are able to address gender-specific challenges, uncover what they are truly capable of, and build the bold and brilliant careers they desire! *Begin Boldly* boils down the most powerful insights that I have learned from working with thousands of women at all career levels around the world. Their main message and mine: The greatest risk for early career women is not taking any risks at all.

"But I'm not experienced enough." "I'm not ready." "I'm just starting my career." Check your excuses at the door! The truth is, I have met hundreds of women who wished they had started making bold moves earlier. I have met none who wished they had waited until later in their careers to take risks.

Why the need to start risk-taking early? My research shows that risks can have compounding returns, so the sooner you start, the better. Imagine a small snowball at the top of a mountain. If you push it off, it will quickly pick up speed, getting bigger and bigger with every turn. This snowball represents the compounding returns of taking risks early in your career. Imagine if you pushed the same snowball off the mountain halfway down. Would it gain as much momentum? Would it have as much time to grow larger? Probably not. If you want great returns, the time to start taking risks is now.

One thing I know with certainty that I wish to impart to you: Brilliant careers are seldom built without bold moves.

....

Your Move to Make

The Story of Nim

Nim De Swardt grew up in Port Douglas, a town in Queensland, Australia, in a treehouse with no windows or doors. Despite this humble and secluded upbringing, she was full of insatiable curiosity about the world and human connections. At the age of thirteen, she took her first flight and began to view travel as the gateway to possibility.

By the time she had turned twenty-five, Nim had taken enormous leaps: leaving home, living in London and Dubai, and traveling to over twenty countries. A chance encounter with the CEO of Bacardi led her to the role of global millennials manager, which then transitioned to chief next generation officer. She moved to Bermuda, a twenty-one-square-mile island in the Atlantic Ocean, where Bacardi Global was headquartered. At thirty years old, she became the youngest direct report to the CEO, forty years her senior. It was a disruptive position, rooted in a dynamic intergenerational partnership between a thirty-year-old risk-taker and a seventy-year-old executive who wanted to ignite change in an organization that was over one hundred and fifty years old.

Nim took multiple risks in her early career. By the time she was thirty-three, she had navigated a wild ride of moving across four different continents; changing departments, industries, and careers; taking two sabbaticals; stepping into a global role at a young age;

negotiating her salary and title; job crafting; launching global programs and transitioning into an intrapreneur; igniting innovation and experimentation within a company; and transforming into a social entrepreneur.

I became Nim's career advisor during her time at Bacardi. When I was coaching her, one thing became overwhelmingly evident. Her appetite for risk set her apart from many of her peers. She had a willingness to push boundaries and to tackle the unknown, based on the faith in her own capacity to figure it all out. For her, a career journey was a wild adventure, a series of continuous experiments, and a process of risking, refining, and reaping rewards. Nim possesses the traits that fuel risk-taking: a deep curiosity about the world and unwavering courage; a penchant for experimentation in life and work; and an ability to adapt quickly. At thirty-six, she is now a lifestorian and the founder of WIN|WIN, an organization that uses the power of human stories to build bridges of empathy and connection across all ages. She is also the cofounder of Tomorrow's Air, an organization that unites travelers to create a stable climate future, and leads growth for Everday Massive, where she transforms the employee experience through human connection.

If Nim had waited until she felt "ready" or for the perfect time, she wouldn't have cultivated the dynamic and multifaceted professional life she has today. By taking risks from day one, Nim was able to learn quickly and craft a bold and brilliant career and life. Feeling ready to take a risk isn't something you can sit around and wait for. Being ready to risk is a decision, one that only you are capable of making.

For Nim, risk-taking was the gateway to growth, an engine to fuel her spirit, infusing her career journey with life, learning, excitement, and experimentation. I include her story in this introduction because I want to share it with others who aspire to live more boldly but may be struggling to take the leap. I have met too many women who played it safe to the detriment of building a career and life they loved. To some of you, Nim may seem like the award-winning marathon runner of risk-taking, while you haven't even laced up your shoes yet. But risk can begin where you are. No matter your starting point, you, too, can learn from Nim and have the courage to explore, dream, and discover your most brilliant career.

Over the last fifteen years, I have worked with and researched thousands of women across the globe. What is the one, core commonality shared among women with bold and brilliant careers? Like Nim, they all embraced risk. Even more important, they started taking risks from day one. Want to build a career you love? The time to take a risk is now.

Why a Book for Early Career Women?

Before we begin our journey in this book, it is worth stating a simple yet disheartening reality: The workplace is not a meritocracy. But not all hope is lost. This book will equip you with the tools to navigate the workplace strategically and successfully, despite challenges and setbacks. Not surprisingly, this requires risk.

I recently ran a global program for early career women at a leading investment firm. At one point, I asked everyone to close their eyes and picture two individuals running a race with the same start line, start time, and finish line. I then asked the group whether this race was fair, and the majority responded with a resounding yes. When they opened their eyes, the audience saw an image on the screen of two races that looked very different. In the left lane was a man in a suit. His lane had two small hurdles in it. In the right lane was a woman with a ball and chain attached to one foot. Her lane had barbwire, tall grass, and terrain to conquer, a wall to climb over, and a swamp to swim through. The caption was "Quit whining. It's the same distance."

The difference in lanes doesn't mean that the male professional doesn't need to run fast, work hard, or overcome some hurdles. It simply means that the race the woman is running is riddled with more obstacles, and she may be held back from the start. These obstacles are even more pronounced for women of color.

Research shows that women go into the workplace equally as

ambitious and confident as their male counterparts. However, early career women:

- Lag behind men in aspiration and confidence by the second year of their careers.[1]
- Report lower levels of job satisfaction.[2]
- Are promoted less often than men.[3]
- Lag behind men in both job level and compensation when they enter the workforce—and never catch up.[4]

According to Lean In and McKinsey's "Women in the Workplace 2019" report, "Women are left behind from the get-go."[5] Their subsequent studies reconfirmed the early career crisis for women, noting that too many women are getting stuck in entry-level jobs. The pandemic has exacerbated the gender divide and created more fissures in the earlier stages of the pipeline, with one in four women reporting that they are contemplating leaving the workplace or downshifting their careers.[6] Despite women facing unique challenges from day one on the job, the lion's share of strategies, programs, and resources still focus on women at more senior levels in their careers. This is too little, too late. Catalyst is a global nonprofit that works with over eight hundred companies around the world to accelerate women in leadership. Catalyst researchers reinforce the importance of the early career years, stating: "When you start from behind, it's hard enough to keep pace, never mind catch up—regardless of what tactics you use."[7]

Compounding the issue is that traditional career advice, based on many of the reasons given to explain the gender gap, doesn't work when women follow it and may actually backfire. For example, take the critique that "women are less likely to negotiate their salaries." In reality, when women try traditional negotiation techniques, it's been shown that not only are they less likely to succeed in the negotiation than a man, but they also face an increased likelihood that their tactics could backfire, with offers being rescinded.[8] No wonder women may be hesitant to negotiate. The harsh truth is that the world reacts to women differently than it reacts to men, and early career women need tools that are calibrated to work for them. This book is your custom tool.

The *Begin Boldly* Solution

Many of these alarming trends are not new. But the actionable solutions I offer here—reimagining risk, embracing uncertainty, and tackling gender barriers—will help you build your brilliant career. This book is infused with the research-driven, real-world strategies that you need to run your best race—and take the risks that will help you win on your own terms. Not all aspects of your career are in your control, but one critical differentiator is: understanding why and, more important, how to take the risks that matter, big or small. The most essential skill to build during your early career years is the *skill of risk-taking*.

The ultimate secret to risk-taking is cultivating the mindsets needed to take the leap. Throughout this book, one of the most important resources I tap is the wisdom, advice, and hindsight of women leaders who have come before you and want to help women like you succeed. Their key piece of advice: Look inward. These women's risk-taking successes were largely a result of their mindsets and inner game. Your inner game directly influences your outer game—your ability to take risks.

Begin Boldly boils down the most powerful insights and effective strategies I have learned from working with women across career levels into a research-backed model featuring three mindsets—a curious mindset, a courageous mindset, an agile mindset—and one essential skill set: risk-taking. This dual approach enables you to take charge of your career from day one. This journey will change the way you think and navigate the world of work and it will help you take the bold risks needed to build a brilliant career.

How to Use This Book

This book is lighter on anecdotes and richer in action. It presents the challenges that women face and an abundance of solutions that you can start implementing in your life now. Tip: If you haven't yet faced some of the challenges in this book, don't dismiss them. They may arise down the road. The key is to go into the workplace with your eyes wide open, looking out for the challenges that may be still to come and feeling empowered by the fact that you have the tools to address them.

Aside from chapters 1 and 2, which give you two foundational frameworks for approaching risks, each chapter in this book covers the following:

- A common **Challenge** women face in the earlier stages of their careers
- A research-driven **Solution** to this challenge
- A **Put-It-into-Practice** section with clearly laid-out techniques to try
- An **Aspiration-to-Action** exercise to help bridge the gap between your aspirations and your actions, which encourages you to adopt a structured approach to experimenting
- A **Risk-Reward-Refine-Repeat** closing that frames how to use these insights to fuel your risk-taking ritual

This book can be used as a comprehensive guide to prepare yourself to make the most of your early career years. It can also be used for those who coach, mentor, counsel, and advise early career women, with insights and exercises for those you are supporting. If you're someone looking to use strategies that are rooted in gender research and that take into account gender differences, this book is for you. This book can also serve as the foundation for a women's program on campuses or in organizations. Want to start a women's group or book club on your campus before you graduate, within your community, or in your organization? You can use this book as your guide— do a chapter per month as you and your group work through the content and activities. Although it was created with the early career woman in mind, women at any stage may find enduring messages and helpful tools. As you face new challenges, you can pull the lever that makes sense for your context.

Despite the continuing barriers faced by women in the workplace, remember: It's not all doom and gloom. It's better to be equipped for success than to gloss over the state of play that still exists, one that's still more challenging overall for women than for men, despite years of progress and the work of generations before us. The inequity exists despite the best intentions of well-meaning leaders and organizations. We have made strides because of these immeasurable contributions and tireless efforts, but not enough has changed to leave our careers up to chance. We must equip ourselves.

Your Move to Make

Some may ask: Why don't we focus on changing society rather than equipping women? Yes, we want the world to transform. Yes, alongside my work with individuals, I advise organizations on changing policies, processes, and cultures that hold women back, on interrupting biases and making tweaks to systems so that we can level the playing field as much as possible and allow women to step into their most successful and meaningful careers. But change isn't happening fast enough. In the absence of the progress that we want, we must prepare ourselves to navigate the world as it is. We can't stand still waiting for norms to be revolutionized without taking our careers into our own hands. This book is not intended to absolve organizations or leaders or society of the responsibility for challenging gender norms and the status quo. It is simply designed to help women navigate the world as it is right now—while we also hope that our organizations are evolving in parallel, ideally with our input.

There are always things that will be frustrating and beyond your control. Go in with your eyes wide open and realize early on that the key to cultivating a brilliant career doesn't lie with others, it lies within you. What if you could crack the code on the skill sets and mindsets that will enable you to thrive in the workplace; to strategically address external boundaries; to move past internal doubt and self-resistance; to navigate the workplace as it is? I challenge you to step into your best career by taking a risk on yourself.

This book is an invitation for you to let go of the fears and beliefs that are no longer serving you and consider what your life could be like if you tackled the tough projects, took on expanded responsibilities, solved the difficult problems, used your voice, and made meaningful connections with those around you. It's an invitation to move from self-defeating inaction to empowered action through intentional and intelligent risk-taking. Working through the practical tools and powerful processes outlined in *Begin Boldly*, you will become equipped to rise to challenges and take chances on yourself. You will infuse your professional journey with energy, adventure, opportunity, and most important, ownership and empowerment. It's time to begin boldly!

PART I

REIMAGINING RISK

....

Do you desire to build a bold and brilliant career? If you picked up this book, your answer is likely "Yes!" Perhaps you dream of taking more chances but don't know where to start. Perhaps you get overwhelmed by overthinking or fear of the unknown. Perhaps you grapple with self-doubt and endlessly analyze worst-case scenarios and outcomes. If any of these are the case, you are not alone and you are in the right place. Women like you, at earlier stages in their career, understand that building a career and life they love is no small feat. Young women are navigating a labyrinth of obstacles, twists, turns, and often dead ends. You probably desire to learn from those who have gone before you as you navigate the ups and downs of your own career journey. However, what I've heard again and again is that the stories of others are not enough. As one early career woman expressed: "We need more than 'this is how I did it.' We need 'this is how you can do it too.'" My fifteen years of work and research in the gender space has uncovered that women aspire to take risks but often struggle to translate that into action. This book is designed to meet the needs of women like you and help you close the gap between your aspirations and your actions by equipping you to take risks in practice. Ask yourself: Do my actions match my aspirations? If not, if you are aspiring to be bolder and braver yet continuing to play it safe, let's build the bridge between what you aspire to do and what you actually take action on. It's time to close that gap and equip you to make bold career moves.

In summary, the secret to building a brilliant career is to take proactive, intelligent risks backed by a plan for a range of possible results, knowing that you can progress no matter the outcome, as long as you possess the right methods and mindsets.

....

CHAPTER 1

Risk–Reward–Refine–Repeat

HAVE YOU EVER SEEN A PHOTO of an accomplished, energized, and vibrant woman in a publication or on social media, or read a ridiculously impressive bio before a conference or on a company website, and asked yourself: "Wow, I wonder how she got there?" The answer consists of one word: risk. Beyond the accolades, accomplishments, and shiny bios of the most inspiring women with whom I've worked are stories of triumph, defeat, trade-offs, tough choices, adversities, setbacks, and lessons learned. Despite their diverse backgrounds and stories, these women who have built bold and brilliant careers all share one core commonality: They seek out and optimize intelligent risks from their first role onward.

Unfortunately, for so many reasons, women enter the workforce believing that they must never make a mistake, and as a result, they see any risk as a bad risk—or overlook the opportunity to risk altogether. The vast majority of early career women I've studied report that they don't seek out or embrace risks. Not only does this result in lost career advancement, it makes taking any single risk seem like the "be all, end all." Risks are not always pivotal, life-altering scenarios; in fact, taking this view of risk makes it even harder to take them. Fabulous careers are built on a comprehensive approach that includes many risks, taken consistently and strategically, that will result in greater advancement overall than a consistent choice to play it safe. Think of your career like an investment portfolio. Yes, taking bigger bets can increase your chance of higher returns. However, you don't just take one big bet. You manage your portfolio on an ongoing basis and take many bets. Think of this like the conventional approach to a portfolio: diversification. You never know how one risk is going to turn out, so you spread the risk over a variety of investments. You can think of every risk you take as an investment in your future, your diversified career portfolio.

Risk-taking is a skill you can learn, refine, and practice until it becomes a habit. It's not a one-off bet or chance. It should be a daily and continuous process of taking an action, a risk; assessing outcomes; refining your approach; and repeating. This is the secret to creating a lasting risk-taking habit: knowing in advance that what you're doing is part of a long-term and ongoing strategy that will yield important rewards, move you forward, and help you grow no matter whether you succeed or fail on each bet.

Learn to See Failure as a Reward

You may be thinking: What if things don't work out as I had hoped? The answer: Even if a risk doesn't have the outcome you hoped for, you can gain exponential growth and insights to fuel your career. An outsized fear of failure is one factor that holds women back from taking risks. However, playing it safe won't expose you to the learning opportunities that come from stretching out of your comfort zone. Taking risks early in your career can help you learn valuable lessons and move ahead more quickly. It can also help you avoid fatal flaws later down the line. Even risks gone wrong can have exponential rewards. You have the opportunity to use the insights and information you gain in a purposeful way to improve and intentionally craft your career path forward. When faced with failure, Kathleen Taylor, chair of the board of the Royal Bank of Canada and former president and CEO of Four Seasons Hotels and Resorts, considers: "What can I learn? What experience can I gain?"[9]

One of the biggest mistakes is thinking that risk-taking has only two outcomes: success or failure, that is, gains or losses. When you take a risk, avoid the faulty assumption that you will either win or lose. This is a forced dichotomy of extremes that holds women back from taking risks. It is true that a failure may lead to some lost ground; a risk is a gamble, and the possibility of a negative outcome is part of the game. But the reward of taking risks is always progress if you optimize risk-taking and have the right mindsets to learn from the outcomes. In all cases, you will either achieve a goal or learn a valuable lesson that will propel you forward and help you refine your approach.

Make It a Habit

Despite struggling to take risks, the majority of women in a recent KPMG study state that people who take more risks progress further in their careers and benefit in other ways too—by developing new skills and earning colleagues' respect.[10] They're not alone in correlating risk-taking with career progression, growth, and credibility. My work and research have highlighted that senior-level women leaders view risk-taking as a continuous practice in their lives and careers. They attribute their success to adopting an adventurous approach to challenges, embracing risk and uncertainty, and having faith in their capabilities to progress regardless of any one given outcome.

Risk-taking is not an isolated action, but rather an ongoing approach to all areas of life, a core aspect of identity. How we think about ourselves has a direct impact on our actions. Flip your script from "I take risks" to "I am a risk-taker." Risk-taking is not a one-off event but a way of living, leading, learning, and infusing energy, optimism, and growth into your career.

This may seem daunting at first. I want to assure you that I am not by any means advocating for a Russian roulette–style approach to your career. However, taking intentional and strategic risks and continuously refining your approach will reap both shorter-term and longer-term career rewards.

The Risk-Taking Ritual

Building any habit is a challenge. Building a risk-taking habit is even more so, since it doesn't come instinctively. It takes practice and repetition, and the best way to do this is with a simple, repeatable framework:

Risk – Reward – Refine – Repeat

The framework is intentionally simple so that you can keep it fresh in your mind; write it down and post it somewhere you can see it. In chapter 2, I introduce you to a more comprehensive model for assessing and preparing for bigger, more involved risks, but as a start, think of Risk-Reward-Refine-Repeat as a mental default setting, a life and career mantra. If you keep coming back to this simple guiding ritual, you will establish a robust risk-taking habit that will help you explore bold possibilities today and for the rest of your career.

By leveraging this approach, you'll be equipped to translate risk-taking aspirations into risk-taking actions, and risk-taking actions into lasting risk-taking rituals that permeate all aspects of your career and life. You'll learn how to identify Risks, assess Rewards, Refine your approaches, and Repeat the cycle with new insights and information. It's a process of continuous improvement that will lead to an enduring and rewarding risk-taking habit.

Numerous career decisions and actions throughout your journey may entail risk:

- Jumping at a challenging assignment or stretch role
- Saying yes to an overseas secondment or temporary assignment
- Seeking a new role or a new organization
- Deciding to go back to school
- Pivoting into a new industry
- Taking a sabbatical
- Putting yourself up for a promotion
- Negotiating your compensation package

- Actively seeking out connections with leaders, mentors, and sponsors
- Raising your hand for high-value and high-visibility projects
- Chairing meetings and making presentations to key leaders
- Taking on new and expanded responsibilities outside your areas of expertise
- Starting an internal initiative or program
- Seeking new learning opportunities outside your comfort zone
- Advocating for yourself and others
- Proposing new ideas, approaches, and uncommon or alternative options
- Applying for a job when you think you don't have all the qualifications

In all cases, you can use the Risk-Reward-Refine-Repeat ritual to view risk-taking as a repeatable process of improvement and growth. To kick-start your risk habit, chapters 3 through 12 each include a Risk-Reward-Refine-Repeat exercise, walking you through the approach so that you'll be well-equipped to use it in your own life.

Risk

The first step is identification: Identify a career risk that you have the choice to take. In this initial step, you find and define a chance in your career that could result in loss or failure. Similar to goal setting, taking a risk begins with clearly identifying an *action* as your starting point. This should be concisely stated in the present tense and framed as an opportunity or choice you can make.

Ask yourself: "What is the career risk I have the opportunity to take?" And define it.

Complete the sentence: *I have the opportunity to . . .*

. . . transition to an expanded career role.
. . . move to another country with my company.
. . . put my name in the ring for a newly created position within my organization.

It may sound obvious, but if you can't identify a risk, you won't be able to successfully take one, and it can be surprisingly hard to do at first. I call the ability to identify risks "honing your risk radar." A poster that reads "Risk is where you least expect it" hangs in Professor Linda Hill's office at Harvard Business School (HBS).[11] Hill currently serves as faculty chair of the Leadership Initiative at HBS. The poster in her room speaks to the fact that risk exists in places you may not have anticipated. This expanded view of risk involves looking for risks that may not immediately be evident.

During the process of producing this book, my editor, Anna Leinberger, shared that in her early career years, she didn't even identify certain critical and career-defining acts as risks that she had the opportunity to take. She thought she had to keep her head down, get the work done, and "not step on people's feet." In hindsight, she reflected that part of the issue was that as woman, we "don't accurately define things as risks." Without this ability to discern what constitutes a risk, important bets, chances, and opportunities are either overlooked or not taken strategically. A *Harvard Business Review* article on gender and risk highlights that we often think about risk in more straightforward, male-dominated ways, such as in physical or financial terms and overlook other types of risk.[12] When discussing risks, many women with whom I've worked also fall victim to these limited definitions and think about risk as it relates to handling finances, starting a business, or becoming an entrepreneur. The author of the article states: "The trouble is that historically risk-taking has been framed so narrowly that it skews our perceptions," which I've found in turn influences women's actions and outcomes.

When women I meet define themselves as "risk-averse," they're often thinking about risk within these narrowly defined terms. Risks aren't reserved for entrepreneurs alone. Risks include speaking up in a toxic culture, advocating for oneself and others, seeking new opportunities, voicing opinions, standing up for what's right despite opposition, and putting your credibility on the line to support others, among other things. With this in mind, you should build your risk radar by thinking about risk in broader terms, and as Linda Hill encourages, look for risk in areas you may least expect it. The most fulfilled women I have met have viewed risk-taking as a daily activity: "It is not just about taking a few big risks but about pushing yourself each day to get outside of your comfort zone."[13] Where fear and discomfort exist, there is likely a risk, a choice to be made. When you feel these emotions, identify the risk you may be overlooking, a career choice that involves a chance of failure or loss, and empower yourself to make a conscious choice about whether to pursue it by using the readiness method described in chapter 2. If you don't take the risk, the process stops here. However, if you take the risk, the next step is to reflect on the rewards.

Reward

Ask yourself: What are the rewards I've experienced as a result of taking this risk? Risking always comes with some sort of reward—whether it be a desired outcome or a lesson learned that will propel your progress. Once you take a risk, the next step is to assess the outcomes and identify the rewards. And remember, "rewards" include both the outcomes of risks that worked out well and outcomes of those that did not. We just need to look at the latter with a new perspective.

Take the example of asking for a critical role on a team project. If you take the risk and are successful, you reap rewards such as achieving your desired outcome—securing the role—and the benefits that come along with that role, such as expanded responsibilities, more exciting tasks, a chance to showcase and further develop your leadership skills, exposure to key executives or clients, or perhaps a chance of earlier promotion.

If you take the risk and are unsuccessful in getting the role, you will still experience rewards. You just need to look at undesired outcomes in a new way. For instance, maybe your manager gave you feedback on why you weren't selected for the role, and this feedback can fuel your learning and growth. Perhaps you differentiated yourself as someone who is ready and willing to take on challenging assignments, and this has resulted in other opportunities coming your way. Perhaps you gained new insights on what matters to your manager and how you can better align your time and energy to those items. Perhaps you gained clarity on what steps you want to take next in your career. All of these rewards will help you progress further in your career than if you hadn't risked at all. This step flips the script from viewing negative repercussions and undesired consequences of risks as failures, instead seeing them as opportunities for growth, continuous improvement, and exponential progress.

When considering potential rewards, think about an extended time frame and take a long-term view: The sooner you start reaping the benefits, the longer the tail of returns that you will receive. Remember the snowball effect discussed in the preface. The longer the snowball is rolling down the hill, the bigger it will become. A simple and tangible example is deciding whether to take a lower-paying offer for a "safe" role or taking the risk of a more expansive and challenging entry-level role with a slight edge on pay. When run through conservative predictive models, a seemingly small difference of $5,000 in starting salary can result in a difference in lifetime earnings of over $1 million. The Federal Reserve Bank of New York's study reinforced this finding, noting that your lifetime earning potential is determined in your twenties.[14] This is one of countless examples that highlight the explicit rewards of risking early. If the risk you have identified is "I have the opportunity to take on a challenging entry-level role with higher pay," the reward might be "I will make more money and move my career forward." The long-term expansion would be, "If I make this leap now, I will get to the next level of my career faster; I might make $10K more this year, but if my next promotion comes more quickly as a result, I could be making $20K more within three years instead of only $10K more." When you add in a compound interest calculation to how much more you could contribute to your retirement savings, you could quantify this one risk into hundreds of thousands of dollars (if not more!) over the course of your career. Each time you take a risk you should complete this sentence: "The rewards I've reaped from taking this risk are ..." Insert any new insights: what you've learned, how you've grown, what progress you've made, what positive outcomes you've experienced, how the experience influenced or affected your thinking and your career.

Remember that some rewards are experienced immediately, others within short time frames, and some come later and are experienced long after one takes the risk. Take an initial assessment of the rewards immediately after risking, but don't forget to revisit this step later on for a second round of reflection, as you may have realized some rewards that were not initially evident or came at a later date.

Refine

Will you let the outcomes of risk-taking define you or refine you? You have the power to ensure that the outcomes of risks, whether desired or undesired, contribute to your continuous evolution and improvement. In the Refine phase, you tweak and enhance your approaches to risk-taking and your career based on what you learned from taking a risk.

Ask yourself: What have I learned from taking this risk that will help me refine my approach to similar situations and other risks in the future?

Think about the example of the risk of putting yourself up for a critical team role. If you weren't successful, perhaps the next time you take a risk you will refine your approach by ensuring that you have an advocate, such as a colleague or former manager, who can speak to your capabilities and skills, or perhaps you could bolster your case by including more talking points on your track record of demonstrated results and impact (more on this to come in the courageous advocacy chapters). If you were successful in getting the role, perhaps you would refine your risk-taking approach in the future by further honing and enhancing some of the tactics you used that worked well so that you can move from strength to strength.

The foundational work on mindsets by the world-renowned Stanford University psychologist Carol S. Dweck highlighted that girls are more likely to see failure or negative outcomes as part of their fixed identity, rather than something to build on or an opportunity to grow.[15] From a young age, girls are more likely to believe that if they take a risk and fail, they are a failure. Why is this so problematic? Because women equate failure, an isolated outcome, with their identity. The internal dialogue is "I failed, therefore I am a failure."

For boys, the internal dialogue is more likely to be "I failed. Failure is data. What can I do to improve?" What my work and research has shown is that this trend for girls continues into adulthood and hinders a woman's ability to take the risks she needs to build a brilliant career. In my study of over 120 women, including women from countries such as the US, UK, Australia, Georgia, Italy, India, Jamaica, Bermuda, Malaysia, Norway, Spain, Switzerland, and Zimbabwe, the most pervasive reason that women did not take risks was fear of failure (77 percent). The key to overcoming this outcome and identity conflation is to understand that failure is not fatal and does not define us. Instead, any outcome of risk—positive or negative—should be used to refine our skills and our approaches to risk-taking in the future. Use the outcomes of risk-taking to refine you—not to define you.

Repeat
The final step in this process: Take more risks. Remember that risk-taking is a skill, and like any skill, it can be honed with practice. Here's the secret about risk-taking: you get better at it only if you do it! While risk-taking is scary and takes courage, taking the risk and managing the outcome builds resilience and skill. The more you do it, the easier it will become. Without a lot of experience taking career gambles, it can be scary to put your cards on the table; however, you can equip yourself to play a strategic game rather than Russian roulette, and then get better with practice. I always tell my clients that "great risk-takers are not born, they are made."

An added bonus: Risk-taking creates a self-perpetuating cycle. You will define yourself as someone willing to go out on a limb, and this identity will increase opportunities that come your way to repeatedly take risks. How we act and behave influences others' impressions of us. By seeking out strategic risks, you send the message to others that you are up for challenges, believe in your capability and skills, and are hungry for more. What I've seen in my work is that even when a risk doesn't have the desired immediate reward, differentiating yourself as a risk-taker can reap long-term reputational rewards. I had a client who was initially unsuccessful in negotiating for an expanded role and adjusted title. However, the act of initiating negotiation highlighted her value, the key aspects of her role, and her appetite for taking risks. It planted the seed in the mind of leadership that this was someone up for a challenge. In less than six months, she was internally recruited for a critical leadership role in the organization. Since she positioned herself as a risk-taker and a changemaker, those around her began to think of her as a candidate for key roles. Risk begets risk: When you make a bold move, regardless of outcome, you will have differentiated yourself as a risk-taker; people will think of you when risks present themselves; more opportunities to take risks will come your way; you take more risks; and the cycle continues. Define yourself as a courageous adventurer, a seeker of new opportunities, someone who is willing to go out on a limb, and someone who is open to exciting challenges. Then you will reap the rewards of repeated risks. What risk are you going to take next?

Let's look at a real-life example of what the Risk-Reward-Refine-Repeat approach looks like in practice.

RISK. After displaying a proven track record of results and having discussions with leadership, Robyn took the risk of going for a promotion at a top-tier consulting firm.

REWARD. She was not successful in securing her desired outcome. Despite the disappointment of not getting a promotion, the decision was a catalyst for her to reflect on and go for what she really wanted. She realized that she was undervalued in her current context. She could have continued in maintenance mode, but she felt that accelerating her career was important, as was being valued for her contributions. The seemingly negative outcome of her risk-taking was a catalyst for these new insights: her rewards.

REFINE. This risk-taking experience refined her outlook on the type of companies she wanted to work for and what was worth risking. She also refined her risk-taking approach, ensuring that she went into future discussions with courage, an understanding of her value and a clear narrative.

REPEAT. She went on to take another risk and apply for a stretch role at the world's leading internet-based companies. She was successful and was hired into a role that was more aligned with her skills and values.

This story wasn't as simple or short as I described above. It took support from others, including a therapist, journaling, and other reflective techniques to dig deep into what she wanted. She also moved back in with her parents in her early thirties and grappled with self-doubt and fears. However, in the end, taking an initial and repeated risk created progress she would not have made by playing it safe.

Get Equipped and Get Going!

In 2016, I was invited to speak at the Women's Forum for the Economy and Society in Normandy, France. I shared the stage with a magnetic and energized social impact entrepreneur, Melody Hossaini, of the same age, thirty years old, and still in the earlier stages of her career. Melody was no stranger to risk. She was the founder and CEO of the social enterprise InspirEngage International, and was best known as a contestant on the seventh season of the BBC television series *The Apprentice*, where she made it to week ten out of twelve. As we stood on the stage in front of an audience, virtual and in-person, of three thousand, she shared that sometimes you may need to go backward to propel yourself forward. Standing on the 360-degree stage, she explained that jumping from her current spot to the other side of the stage was difficult, particularly in heels and a dress, and asked how she could jump farther. Then she backed up and, with a running start, made a longer leap. "If you want to go really far, go back first and then charge forward," Melody said. "The challenges and failures we face in life are these steps back that allow us to go further than we would have if we just started from here—but only if you allow that to become a part of your journey."

That journey involves making Risk-Reward-Refine-Repeat a habit, an enduring ritual in your career and life. The practice isn't just about taking one big leap but rather about taking many leaps over the course of your career. Think back to the example at the beginning of this chapter of developing an investment portfolio. Like a traditional investment portfolio, your career portfolio requires ongoing management, continual investment, and diversified risks. It isn't a one-and-done scenario; it's a continuous way of living. We all have the power to take risks and adopt a Risk-Reward-Refine-Repeat ritual of behavior in our careers. We just need the right tools and the right mindsets, as outlined in this book. We just need to get equipped and get going.

CHAPTER 2

Take Strategic Risks Boldly

ONCE YOU HAVE GRASPED the Risk-Reward-Refine-Repeat ritual, you may be thinking "How do I do step one: taking the risk?" This chapter is your answer. It is about the most important step of the ritual: actually making that first leap! Imagine you are preparing for a mountain climb, a challenging hike, or a long journey over rough and uncertain terrain. You wouldn't venture into the wilderness without a proposed path, navigation devices, a plan if things go awry, and a safety net or emergency contact. Your career should be no different. In this chapter, you will be introduced to a method that will serve as your tool kit for exploring the amazing and exciting terrain of risk-taking.

Exploring Uncharted Waters

Many women shy away from risks because they don't have a formula for identifying them, assessing them, taking action, and dealing with the outcome, whether desired or undesired. Without such a method, the daunting unknowns and uncertainty hold them back. When I asked women in the first ten years of their careers to complete the sentence "For me risk-taking is...," many responded with themes of the unknown:

"Leaving a comfortable environment for the unknown."
"Taking an unexpected approach where the outcome is unknown."
"Venturing into the unknown."
"Walking into the unknown."

"Exploring the unknown."

Uncharted waters can seem scary in comparison to the safety of a harbor. A fear of the unknown can disincentivize risk-taking just as much as a fear of failure. In the career context, too many of us favor the comfort of certainty over the discomfort of the unknown. Many of the women I've worked with over the years express that a barrier to risk-taking is the desire to focus on what they can control, instead of facing uncertainty.

To begin with, it's important to recognize that we take risks and face uncertainty in other areas of life, and the lessons from these realms can be applied to our professional trajectories.

Think about it: We take risks all the time. Getting in your car is a risk. You have the chance of a negative outcome—an accident—yet most people don't think twice about their decision to drive, and do it daily. The important difference here is that you generally know how to drive a car. You know what the roads are like, what all the signs mean, how your machine functions. You even know generally what the possible bad outcomes could be, and a little of what to do in those situations. Your driver's ed class probably taught you some safe-driving and defensive techniques, and you have access to maps or GPS. You have car insurance. You have your manual in your glove compartment. You have the phone number of a service to fix a flat, tow your car, or help you in the event of an accident. You have the tools and techniques to navigate the uncertainty associated with taking this risk.

Career risks are scary because often we don't have any road map and we don't have the tools and techniques to deal with possible outcomes. So instead of a risk like getting into your car, taking a career risk often feels more like being told "There are amazing rewards for you if you go take that paraglider over there and fly it to the bottom of that cliff. Oh and you have to do it blindfolded." Now, maybe you know how to paraglide, but it's safe to assume that most people don't. You don't know where you're going to land; you don't know what might be around the next corner. You don't even know with any level of specificity what the possible rewards are. The method in this chapter provides you with a road map for risk-taking.

The Bold MOVES Method for Strategic Risk-Taking

To take bold leaps, the solution is to equip yourself with a method to prepare for the first step in the Risk-Reward-Refine-Repeat ritual and manage uncertainties and outcomes, both good and bad. When deciding whether to take a risk, you don't need to jump off a cliff and fly blind. Instead, you can take intelligent risks and embrace uncertainty by being equipped with the Bold MOVES method to help you build your strategy and to prepare for action, uncertainties, and possible outcomes.

Bold MOVES

Motivation
What is your motivation?

Opportunity
What is the opportunity? What are the potential opportunity costs?

Vision
What is your future vision for the best case scenario outcome?

Endgame Plan
What is your endgame plan if things go well? What is your endgame plan if they don't?

Support
Who is your support? Identify your stakeholders, success advisers, and safety net.

With a distinct method for approaching risk-taking, you can address any fear or overwhelming anxiety associated with the unknown and continue to adopt your enduring Risk-Reward-Refine-Repeat ritual in your life. Remember to think about this ritual as a behavior or habit, an overall approach to your career, and the Bold MOVES method as a distinct way to assess and prepare for a specific risk in that first step of your ritual.

To begin boldly, you can trade your fear of the unknown for the excitement of endless possibilities with the knowledge that you are going to progress regardless of outcome. As Nim shared: "I risk for the thrill of the unknown, with trust that growth lies on the other side." The key to embracing uncertainty like Nim did is having a method to help you prepare to take intelligent risks and manage a range of possible outcomes, knowing you will grow. As you progress through this book, you'll learn the methods to improve your risk-taking readiness, embrace uncertainty, tackle tough outcomes, and build your brilliant career.

How to Use the Bold MOVES Method

Use the Bold MOVES method to assess career-related risks, including when you're considering whether to take a new job, or when you're making a career pivot or change. This method could also help you assess whether to take the risk of creating an online platform to raise awareness on an issue you care about and putting your views into the public domain. It could help if you have an idea for a new product and are trying to decide whether to pitch it to your boss. It could help if you're debating whether or not to take on an international assignment. These are just a few examples of many situations where you can apply this method. Once you have identified the risk—the opportunity in front of you—use these five steps to prepare.

Motivation

Answer the question: "What is my 'why'?" In other words, "What is my motivation for taking this risk?" Crystallizing your 'why' will fuel your capacity to risk.

In addition, this step encourages you to ask yourself: Does the motivation fit the risk? If your motivation is strong and clear, the risk will be worth exploring further. However, if you feel that you're taking an outsized risk in relation to a weak or questionable motivation, then you may want to reconsider. Figure out what is important to you and crystallize a motivation that really matters. If it doesn't really matter, it won't really motivate.

A red flag to look for is a motivator that is based solely on comparisons with others or the perceptions of others. The trap of comparison is easy to fall into in your early career years, especially in the age of social media. Kathleen Taylor, former president and CEO of Four Seasons Hotels and Resorts, shared this piece of advice for early career women: "Resist the urge to look sideways at your peer group for benchmarking. Make your benchmark internal. Set your own personal benchmarks. You can't have it all, but you can have your all."[16] In other words, invest in what matters to you and aim to improve your internal benchmarks, your own point of reference against which you are comparing and assessing your progress in those areas of personal importance. Don't rely heavily on an arbitrary external benchmark or comparison with others. I often work with women who are benchmarking themselves against a co-worker or talking about their lives in comparison to their peers; however, they rarely know the inner workings of others' careers and lives. Successful women suggest looking inward to isolate your own powerful motivators. Figure out what's important to you and crystallize a motivation that really matters. Remember: If it doesn't really matter, it won't really motivate. To take this a step further, if you don't have a motivation that matters, the risk of undesirable outcomes increases, since you'll be less committed to taking the risk fully and intentionally. Rather than falling victim to the curse of comparison, especially pervasive in our ever-connected world with the lives and highlight reels of others so visible, ensure your motivation is grounded in your own goals.

Opportunity

Risk has traditionally been viewed negatively, with a focus on how to manage, hedge, or mitigate it. This book is inviting you to reimagine risk entirely. Many women report that the thought of taking a risk is anxiety inducing or even terrifying. If you have ever been scared to take a risk, you are not alone. By contrast, many of the senior-level women I've met explain that they have innovative perspectives on risk. One woman shared: "Where other people might see risk, I have always also seen opportunity inside the risk."[17] In short: Women who successfully risk refer to risk with different language.

Language and framing can elicit different emotional responses, which directly influence behavior and appetite for taking chances. By tweaking the language, you can increase your probability of taking action. Reimagining risks as opportunities or bold moves is empowering, exciting, and entices action.

Instead of stating that "Putting myself up for promotion is a risk," you can reframe this as "I have the opportunity to make the bold move of putting myself up for promotion." "Changing careers is a risk" becomes "I have the opportunity to change careers." "I am going to risk negotiating my pay" becomes "I have the opportunity to ask for a package that more accurately reflects my value." What is your opportunity statement? Are you taking the risk of managing a high-profile project at your company, or do you have the opportunity to make a bold move? Crafting your opportunity statement will help you move past unfounded or overstated fears based on language and framing, view risks as a choice that you as the owner of your career can make, and help you hone in on whether this is a bold move worth making.

On the other side of opportunity there is opportunity cost. Time is not infinite, and all decisions have trade-offs. Everything to which you say yes will have an opportunity cost. Although we often hear about opportunity cost as it relates to the economics of investments, here we are using the term to represent the potential opportunities and benefits that you may need to forgo if you choose a bold move. Understanding this allows for better decision-making. What might you need to say no to if you pursue this opportunity? What might you no longer have time for? What other opportunities will you have to forgo? What aren't you leaving room for? Facing these costs upfront is important. After crafting your opportunity statement, it is important to answer: What are the potential opportunity costs of making this bold move? Be intentional about it. Ensuring that you understand and can accept the trade-offs is essential to smart and strategic risk-taking.

Vision

It's helpful to close your eyes and picture: If this works out, what am I doing, saying, feeling, surrounding myself with? Creating a vision helps anchor you to what's possible instead of hyperfocusing on the worst-case scenario. In my experience working with women, a barrier to reaping the rewards of risk is catastrophizing, or catastrophic thinking. This occurs when we assume the worst-case scenario or believe that things are much worse than they actually are. Have you ever focused on everything that could go wrong instead of what could go right? Have you ever played out every worst-case scenario in your head? These tendencies or cognitive distortions create barriers to intelligent risk-taking because risks seem much larger than they really are and appear harder to handle than they are in reality. Research proves that the human brain is wired to overestimate the size of a risk.[18] One powerful way to counteract this tendency is to flip the script from "What is the worst that could happen?" to "What is the best that could happen?" This is what my research has isolated as the most powerful catalyst for an increased appetite for risk. In my research study, I asked: "If you have ever taken a risk, what factors/ reasons contributed to this?" Ranked number one was "excitement regarding best-case outcome," with over 70 percent of respondents highlighting this as reason to risk. Ask yourself: What's the best that could happen? Create the vision for your ideal outcome. Visualize the reward. Be descriptive, make it vivid, and return to that as a driver in decision-making.

When assessing risk, ask yourself: Is this vision worth the risk? It's easy to get so consumed with the climb that we can lose sight of whether we are truly excited about the destination. The popular illustrators Liz and Mollie created an image of someone climbing a ladder. The caption next to one of the bottom rungs said: "If you're going to spend a lot of time here"; the caption next to the top of the ladder said: "Make sure you're excited about this part, too."[19] This message is incredibly powerful. If your long-term future vision doesn't excite you, you may need to evaluate whether the risks at the beginning of your climb are worth it. If not, you may need to find a different ladder to a different destination, one that you truly desire.

Endgame Plan
This book is not about minimizing the chances of a negative outcome or loss. It's about proactively preparing for a range of outcomes. Rather than trying to reduce the risk of failure, you would be better off putting your energy into creating a plan for failure. If you've never failed, you aren't taking bold enough risks. Women who have successfully taken risks have a few philosophies that they

rely on. One is to always have a backup plan. If the risk doesn't work out, they have ideas on how they can course correct, whether it's switching companies, going back to a previous position, or tapping into their savings and support network. They consider what they can do to improve the situation if their risk doesn't go well.

As you prepare to take a risk, answer these questions: What am I going to do if this works? What am I going to do if it doesn't?

Think of different scenarios and what your options may be. You don't need to solidify all the details of a specific plan, but have options that you feel comfortable exploring if things fall through. If things go well, ensure that you're prepared to rise to the occasion and create a plan to position yourself for success.

Remember that having a plan is not at odds with being adaptable, flexible, and agile (see part 4). The world's most successful women have a vision and plan but are also open to change, evolution, growth, and new opportunities. Planning for different outcomes is an important part of preparing for risk; however, you must be open to revising your plans based on the context at hand.

If you plan ahead for the possible outcomes, you are taking an intelligent risk! Should you lose ground or take steps back, that's okay. If you have prepared for it and have a contingency plan, you will still make progress that you wouldn't have made if you were playing it safe.

Support

Women who take risks intelligently have another secret to their success: If possible, don't go it alone. They recognize the important role others play in their careers; no woman is an island and our connectivity and relationships are critical to our successes. Many successful risk-takers highlight that having that support is particularly important when proposing initiatives or ideas that others may view as outside the box. One lawyer shared: "When you want to push the envelope, bring people along."[20] Don't be on a stand-alone platform.

When preparing to take a risk, it is important to think about support in three ways.

STAKEHOLDERS. First, who in your life will be affected by your decision and the potential outcomes of the risks? These are your critical stakeholders, and they should be consulted when you are deciding to take a risk. It could be your manager, a peer or colleague, a partner or family member. Many senior female leaders have encouraged conscious and collaborative decision-making when it comes to taking on risks, with one saying: "Prioritize that promotion or new job opportunity in a discussion with your partner and family. Don't forget that if you get a new job, everybody in your house gets a new job....Everybody has a different life because you have changed yours. What are you going to do differently to support the change and help to make it work?"[21] Similarly, if you take on more responsibilities or a new project, your team may be affected, and everyone's daily tasks might look different. Communicating is key. You'll learn in the chapters that follow how to figure out what matters most to the people who matter to you and how to use curiosity to build buy-in from individuals during critical conversations around risk-taking.

SUCCESS ADVISERS. Second, who are your risk-taking success advisers whom you can consult as you decide whether to take a leap? External counsel can be helpful, especially from those who have risked and reaped the rewards in their careers. You should seek success advisers who have pushed boundaries professionally and taken chances on themselves. Remember that when it comes to risk-taking, success advisers aren't just the ones who have risked and received the benefits. They are also individuals who have failed, leveraged those lessons for growth and progression, and continued to risk. Remember to be clear that you are the ultimate decision-maker and that you're asking others to provide valuable input but not make the call. Align yourself with risk-takers and learn from them. Bonus: You will be closer to where the risks happen and will increase the probability of people associating you with bold and brave women, as well as sending career-defining opportunities your way.

SAFETY NET. Your safety net might involve individuals who are stakeholders and those who are your success advisers, but it may also include other individuals, such as colleagues, peers, mentors, and sponsors. Your net is composed of the individuals who will help you course correct when things go awry and also help you make the most of the positive outcomes of risk when things go well. They provide you with the security and support you need to make good things happen on the back end of taking risks. Imagine you put yourself up for a role that's outside your comfort zone. Your safety net will help you rise to the challenge if you get the role. If you don't, your safety net will help you recalibrate and refocus on what you learned and how to move forward. The latter is particularly important, because my research and experience have shown that women are penalized more harshly for making mistakes than men, and that Black women, Indigenous women, and other women of color face the harshest consequences for failures and mistakes. Despite the fact that you may face disproportionate repercussions for risk in comparison with your male peers, all hope is not lost. The solution here is investing in developing your support, in particular the people comprising your safety net, who can help soften the blows of inequitable and biased repercussions to risk, help you make the most of your lessons, advocate for you with others, and maintain your risk-taking momentum.

Doug Sundheim, the author of *How to Take Smart Risks*, states: "Women are perceived to be more risk averse. That means that women are at a disadvantage when it comes to getting support for risk-taking."[22] This is why the *S* in the Bold MOVES method is so important: you will need to be incredibly intentional in building your support, more intentional than your male colleagues. With the right support in place—stakeholders, success advisers, and a safety net—you can strategically move from the path of least resistance to the path of intentional risks and reap the rewards.

If you're struggling to find the support you need, don't let that halt your best-laid plans for risk. Your support system may come from unexpected places: friends, peers, colleagues, former class-mates, coaches, professors, advisers, and others outside your imme-diate workplace team. The tools and techniques you'll learn in part 2, on curiosity, will help you connect with others and build the rela-tionships that matter to form this support network.

Making an Intelligent and Intentional Decision on Risk

Once you've used this method to assess the risk at hand, answer: Are you going to make the bold move? Why or why not? Leveraging this method will not only make you a smarter risk-taker but also ensure that each decision you make to avoid a risk is intentional and defen-sible, not solely based on fear of the unknown.

When preparing to take a risk, use the letters from the word *MOVES* to guide your decision-making, help you overcome your fear of uncertainty, and create a decisive plan for action. Assess your Motivation, Opportunity, Vision, Endgame Plan, and Support. What bold moves are you going to make to unlock your best self and best career?

....

CHAPTER 3

Build Your Risk Resilience

ADOPTING A RISK-REWARD-REFINE-REPEAT approach to your life and career does not come without challenges that could throw you off course and delay or prevent you from achieving your Vision. The solution is to build your risk resilience so that you can take on any obstacles that stand in your way. Imagine you're venturing out again on your risky expedition. You're leaving the safety of a harbor to sail into open and uncertain seas. The best preparation isn't a map or navigation guide that tells you that everything will be smooth sailing. Instead, the best guide is one that tells you where the shallow waters are, where you could run ashore, and where the reefs are that could sink the ship of even the most skilled sailor. Risk-taking is no different. We need to go in with our eyes wide open, planning for what could hold us back, and using a map or guide to circumvent those obstacles. Even with the best-laid plans and a method to prepare for taking strategic risks, there will still be challenges along the way. You must be equipped to address these barriers when they arise, including internal obstacles—like self-doubt and your inner critic—as well as the inevitable external obstacles.

/ **Challenge** / *Risking doesn't come without roadblocks, and these diversions can easily set women off the course of risk.*

No one ever said risking was going to be easy: Taking risks involves overcoming obstacles along the way. Unfortunately, some of these hurdles can easily divert women from continuing on their bold journeys.

It's easy to get sidetracked on your road to risk. Sometimes a failed first attempt leads to "aspirational collapse," when we give up too readily because our initial outcomes don't align with our original aspirations. In other cases, women report self-doubt and their inner critic taking hold. They may not feel ready to risk or are not sure that they're capable of risking and dealing with the outcomes. We focus on what we can lose or what might go wrong while underestimating our ability to handle changes. Women are more prone to doubt their abilities,[23] and this leads them to be less willing to take a risk, a bet, or a chance. My work has reinforced that women continually underestimate their ability to rise to the challenges that risk, change, and uncertainty produce.

/ **Solution** / *Cultivate the motivations and mindsets for resilience.*
The key to overcoming these obstacles is building your risk resilience so that you can continue on the path to progress. When faced with something that could set you off course, you will have a choice of whether to continue on the path to progress or take detours to a safer but less-rewarding route.

Your inner game (your motivations and your mindsets) influences your outer game (your appetite and ability to risk). Initial disappointment over desired outcomes that didn't materialize, fear of failure, self-doubt, and other roadblocks to risk can all be interrupted by motivations and mindsets!

Put It into Practice

Be curious, courageous, and agile in the face of setbacks and challenges. Through cultivating your curiosity, courage, and agility, you will unleash your enduring risk-taking skill set. The rest of the book is dedicated to exploring these three mindsets and showing you how to learn them and leverage them to take intentional risks. The three mindsets that are critical to a successful and bold career are:

A CURIOUS MINDSET. Being curious will help you overcome fears of networking and enable you to build your powerful Support network. It will also help you navigate the gender bind and wield influence in situations where you are making an ask and taking a risk. Finally, it helps address a critical barrier to risk-taking: "competing priorities." While curiosity can't give you more hours in your day, it can help you make the most of those hours so that you can reduce feelings of conflict and take more strategic risks.

A COURAGEOUS MINDSET. Focusing on courage instead of confidence will enable you to move past inaction due to lack of confidence and to take strategic risks with small courageous acts, while advocating for yourself and others.

AN AGILE MINDSET. Through focusing on agility, you will be able to view yourself and your capabilities and skills as fluid, not fixed, and understand that you're on a lifelong journey of continuous improvement. You'll be able to view your life and career as being in a constant state of experimentation and design, to view your identity as malleable and flexible, and to view change as a catalyst for your ongoing improvement and growth.

Refocus on your motivation to maintain momentum. The Motivation in the Bold MOVES method is key to building your risk resilience. When facing aspirational collapse, self-doubt, and fear, you can turn to one of the best tried-and-true tactics: Return to your 'why.' Motivation maintains momentum. Doubt and fear are unavoidable in building a career that is bold and brilliant. The question isn't whether we will feel these emotions but how we will recognize them and make progress despite them. One of the best tactics for getting through times of doubt is to refocus on your 'why.' This is conveyed in one of my favorite quotes by the philosopher

Friedrich Nietzsche: "[S]he who has a strong enough why can bear almost any how." What is your 'why'? Return to this as your anchor whenever you're struggling with fear and self-doubt during the risk-taking process. If your 'why' is worth it, the how becomes easier. If you have crafted a motivation that matters, it will help you overcome roadblocks to risk-taking.

A successful execution of risk can only follow from a deep understanding of why you are risking. For me, this was a critical grounding force when I grappled with fear and self-doubt in my career. After I left a Big 4 consulting firm and launched my own business, I convinced myself that I didn't need to create a website, publish, or have a public presence to do good business. I had a robust client pipeline, and the excuse that I used was that the purpose of all those things was to build demand, which I already had. But once I dug deeper, I realized that my excuse didn't stand up to scrutiny. The real reason was that I was afraid of putting myself into the public realm, where I would be open to critique. What got me beyond that fear was recentering on my 'why.' I knew that my 'why' was that I wanted to equip women to lead bold and brilliant lives and to support leaders in creating dynamic and vibrant organizations where women could rise. By playing it safe and small, I restricted my ability to have a broader impact. My 'why' was strong enough for me to overcome my fears. Once I refocused on my 'why,' a whole world of opportunity (and yes, risk!) opened up to me. Within the next year, I published two *Harvard Business Review* articles on women in the workplace, one of which was featured as *HBR*'s most popular article and selected as one of its top articles on diversity, and I was honored with a Thinkers50 Radar Award and shortlisted for the biannual Thinkers50 Talent Award. Before those doors could open, I had to get my head in the game by refocusing on my 'why.'

Many women share similar stories, stating that inspiration can come from within and that you must take time to tap into your personal motivations and leverage inner inspiration as your drive. Leena Nair, former chief human resources officer (CHRO) of Unilever and recently appointed CEO of Chanel, grew up in a small town in India and was the first girl in her family to have the opportunity to attend a school that taught English and had a formal curriculum. Each day, she cycled twenty-four miles to get to her school and back. Years later, as a leading executive, her motivation drives her appetite for risk. "I am very centered on my purpose. My purpose is about igniting the human spark in everyone to build a better business and a better world."[24] To achieve this goal, risk is required.

The Trifecta of Risk-Taking

The difficult truth is that strategic risk-taking does not come without challenges that could lead to diversions. Instead, it requires knowing what might get in your way and proactively preparing for that by mastering your inner game—your motivation and your mindsets. To be a successful risk-taker, you have to acknowledge the prospect of undesired outcomes and know that with the right mindsets and tools you will grow!

There are three components to intercepting obstacles that might derail your bold and brilliant career. As covered in part 1, these include:

1— A risk-taking ritual (Risk-Reward-Refine-Repeat) to guide your behavior, make risk-taking a habit, and apply your learnings and progress

2— A method to assess risk readiness, prepare for action, and prepare for a range of possible outcomes (Bold MOVES method)

And coming in parts 2, 3, and 4 is the third pillar of risk-taking:

3— The right mindsets (a curious mindset, a courageous mindset, an agile mindset) for risk-taking reslience

This book provides you with the techniques and tools you need to build and implement all three components in your career and life.

It's time to explore your bold possibilities and cultivate the mindsets that matter.

Aspiration-to-Action

At the end of each of the remaining chapters in this book, you'll have the opportunity to complete an Aspiration-to-Action exercise and adopt a Risk-Reward-Refine-Repeat approach so that it becomes a ritual. For this initial section, we're going to start off with a summary reflection to lay the foundation for the following chapters. If you're reading this with a group, such as a book club or women's group on campus or within your organization, or you know someone also reading this book, consider identifying a *Begin Boldly* accountability advocate. This person will share the journey with you and will help hold you accountable for translating the insights in this book into actions in your own career and life. And you'll do the same for them!

Reflect on a bold move you have taken in the past. Perhaps it was taking on a challenging assignment or a stretch role, putting yourself up for promotion or requesting an accelerated promotion time frame, negotiating your compensation package, taking on new and expanded responsibilities outside your area of expertise, applying for a job when you didn't think you had all the qualifications, publishing an article or post on a topic of interest, starting an initiative or program at your organization or university, taking on a student leadership role, or leading an employee group. If you're struggling to identify a bold move that you have taken in the past, ask a close friend, colleague, mentor, coach, or family member to help you reflect. Ask them: When was a time I took a risk or made a bold move in my education or career? When did I take a chance that had a probability of loss or failure? Even if you don't define yourself as a risk-taker, even if you feel like you play it safe more often than not, there most likely are select situations where you pushed yourself outside your comfort zone.

Complete the sentence: *The bold move I took in the past was...*

Reflect on the following questions.

Motivation. What were your motivations at the time you made this move?

Opportunity. What was the opportunity? What were the potential opportunity costs?

Vision. What was your future vision for the best-case scenario outcome? If you didn't have one at the time, capture what you believe could have been possible if things worked out well.

Endgame Plan. Did you have an endgame plan? If not, describe what your endgame plan could have been. If you did, capture what it was. What was your endgame plan if things went well? What was your endgame plan if they didn't?

Support. Who was your support? Identify your stakeholders, success advisers, and safety net (regardless of whether you utilized their support). If you didn't leverage the support of others, whom could you have engaged?

···················· **Risk-Reward-Refine-Repeat** ····················

Risk. Reflect on the above risk you took. Capture it to serve as the foundation for your Risk-Reward-Refine-Repeat reflection. *The bold move I took in the past was...*

Reward. Thinking back on the risk you took, reflect on the outcomes. Did your risk-taking have your desired outcome? If yes, what rewards did you experience? Did this catalyze your growth or push you farther than you would have gone if you hadn't risked? If not, did you face loss or feel a sense of failure? What did you learn? Did your outcome give you new insights, build resilience, bring other opportunities your way, or result in you pivoting in a way you perhaps didn't expect? If you feel that you didn't internalize the rewards enough at the time, use this reflection time to consider what the rewards were in hindsight.

Refine. How did you refine your outlook and approaches moving forward? Did you take any of the learnings and refine your approach to risk or to your career? If not, how can you use the insights you now have in hindsight to refine your approach to taking risks in the future?

Repeat. Have you repeated risks since this time? If yes, what bold moves did you make? If not, don't worry! The rest of the journey in this book will give you countless opportunities to repeat risks and hone your enduring risk-taking ritual.

PART II

THE CURIOUS MINDSET

·········

It's not uncommon for women to put undue pressure on themselves to have all the answers in their daily working environments, to always have something to say or a point of view to share, and then to feel overwhelmed when they don't. However, the key to taking strategic risks isn't having all the answers or always having something to say. Instead, it's about approaching your career with a curious mindset and always having something to ask. Swap your focus on answers to a focus on asks, and supercharge your risk-taking skill set.

When interviewing such leaders as Leena Nair and Betsy Myers, a former senior adviser to President Bill Clinton and President Barack Obama, I was struck by their insatiable curiosity that fueled an inquiry-based approach to all human interactions. These phenomenal women are prime examples of individuals who ask as many questions about you as they answer about themselves. Similar to Nim, curiosity was a cornerstone of their existence. Curiosity about the world and those around them fuels their day-to-day approaches to life and work. The women I've met and interacted with over the years, those who have crafted the most brilliant careers, embody a spirit of curiosity that touches everyone they meet. They have a hunger for knowledge, meaningful connections, and lifelong exploration and discovery. They ask the tough questions and display an unwavering commitment to understanding others. They are inquisitive listeners, question-askers, and self-described "perpetual students." Like Betsy, Leena, and Nim, their lives, careers, and appetites for risk-taking are shaped by a curious mindset. Curiosity marks their approach to their careers, resulting in ongoing opportunities for new learning and ideas, and most important, strategic risk-taking. The amazing thing about cultivating a curious mindset in your early career years is that it means you don't have to have all the answers, you just need to harness the power of curiosity to ask the right questions and, in turn, unleash your potential to risk intelligently.

CHAPTER 4

Cultivate Connectivity through Curiosity

GOING BEYOND YOUR COMFORT ZONE to connect with new people can feel like a risk in your early career years. The fear of invites ignored, of outright rejection, of conversations that fall flat, of awkward silences, and of mentorships that don't materialize can be a hindrance to building the connections that matter most. But connecting with others, even in the face of discomfort and potential failure, is usually a risk worth taking. The long and the short of it: Connectivity is correlated with career success. A research study by Catalyst, and countless others studies, notes that networking is a key factor that enables women to progress.[25] The question isn't whether we need to connect with others but how we are going to connect in meaningful ways. The answer: Connect with curiosity.

When I work with women in the earlier stages of their career, few things elicit as much fear as the dreaded word *networking*. Have you ever shied away from attending a networking event? Have you ever walked into a room and your chest tightens, hands sweat, and nerves heighten? Have you ever tirelessly prepared for what you were going to say on a call and then still struggled to articulate your thoughts without sounding awkward? Have you ever beaten yourself up after an event because what you meant to say just didn't come out right? Does networking ever feel almost underhanded, as you think about all the things you need or want to get from others? At best, most of us are a little uncomfortable networking; at worst, we find even the thought of networking to be cringeworthy, forced, and anxiety provoking. In this chapter, I'm going to share the one simple tool you need to cultivate the connections that matter most.

Applying a lens of curiosity to those around us is a simple and often-overlooked technique for building meaningful connections with others. When networking, early career women are often ill-advised to hyperfocus on what they want to say instead of crafting something equally, if not more, important: what they want to ask.

Research shows that questions in conversation have the power to increase likability and build more authentic connections with people while helping address the pervasive pressure and often accompanying fears of networking.[26] Relationships are at the core of the human experience both inside and outside the workplace. To fully engage with other people, we must adopt a spirit of inquiry and infuse curiosity into our conversations.

/ **Challenge** / *Many early career women report that they shy away from one of the most essential career-building activities, networking, due to anxiety and fears. This becomes career limiting, especially at later stages in their careers.*

Why is connectivity important? Because the strength of your networks can directly influence your long-term career prospects. We have decades of data proving that the right connections are correlated with better career outcomes (including but not limited to getting your foot in the door for new roles and advancing within organizations). Many studies have correlated the power of networks with someone's career mobility and career advancement; as one example, the work by Boris Groysberg at Harvard has highlighted that women who have built amazing careers succeed by leveraging their broad networks.[27]

On the flip side, one often-cited and well-documented reason that more female managers don't advance to top executive roles is their lack of established informal organizational and industry networks.

My research with Lauren Noël, also reinforced this theme: Women who have crafted meaningful and fulfilling careers possessed a *collective* focus and shared the belief that no woman is an island, and that our connectivity and relationships are absolutely critical to our success. In other words: Don't go at it alone![28]

Why start early? Connectivity breeds connectivity, so starting early is essential if you want to reap compounding returns. The one mistake I see women making again and again is waiting until they feel they need a network to start cultivating connections. If you wait until you're ready to transition roles or organizations to build your network, it's too little, too late. Building meaningful connections should happen before you have a distinct need. By starting earlier, you can maximize what I term the multiplier effect of networking. You connect with one person, who connects you with two others, they connect you with four others, and it continues. Your network expands and expands through this knock-on effect. The time to network is now so that you can reap the multiplier effect of network returns during your entire career.

/ **Solution** / *Use curiosity as a tool for tackling fears and hesitations around connecting with others.*

Imagine having dynamic and vibrant networks and meaningful connections with people who infuse value and insight into your career as you do the same for others. The key to bridging the gap between where you are and where you want to be is to use curiosity as a tool for tackling fear and hesitation around connecting with others. You have the ability to harness the power of questions in conversation to build connections. Again, it's about focusing on flipping the script: Instead of thinking about what you want to say, think about what you want to ask, including what you want to learn or know.

In the summer of 2019, I developed and delivered a weeklong class, *She Leads: A Real World Readiness Program,* for female students in their final years of high school. Designed to help bridge the gap between what we learn in school and what skill sets and mindsets are required outside the classroom, the program addressed a range of topics, including a lecture titled "Nerves and Networking: Making the Connections That Matter." What did the students put into practice to address their fears? They approached networking with a spirit of inquiry—that is, a curious mindset. When they shifted the focus from preparing what they wanted to say to what they wanted to ask, the nerves associated with networking were noticeably reduced. I've used this tool again and again with women I coach, mentor, and advise. The bonus: You will learn exponentially from the experiences and insights of others at a critical growth period of your career. Curiosity is the foolproof solution we all can use to ignite connectivity while moving past our fear and hesitation.

Put It into Practice

Reframe networking. Contrary to popular belief, language matters. How we label an activity matters. Different words elicit different reactions, so how we frame something can have differing psychological and behavioral impacts. In one experiment, some people were asked to think about making friends at a cocktail party and others were told to imagine trying to network and make professional connections. Those who were in the networking group responded that they felt "dirty," including feeling self-serving, manipulative, or deceitful, and shied away from connecting with others. My work and research have revealed that the association between networking and "dirtiness" arises more in women. Given that women are more prone to worry about being "liked" than their male peers, it isn't surprising that we may shy away from networking if we feel that it is self-serving and could affect likability.[29]

How do we reduce the negative feelings associated with networking? We can use different language. Use the power of reframing to position it as "connecting with others" or "building meaningful relationships with others" or "forging new friendships" or "cultivating connections" or "getting to know others." Find the words that work for you and reduce those feelings of "ickiness" and angst.

Adopt a curious mindset and focus as much on what you want to ask as on what you want to say. In 2016, I gave a lecture at the University of Oxford's Saïd Business School on the future of work and reigniting human connectivity in organizations. I shared an image of an iceberg, noting that what we see above the waterline is only about 10 percent of a person and that the key to building powerful connections is seeking to understand the person behind the work, the other 90 percent. As you think about connecting with others, prepare questions that will allow you to do that, to get beneath the surface. Seek to understand the person behind the work.

Not long after this lecture, in early 2017, I was co-facilitating a program for early career women hosted by Harvard Business School (HBS). Alison Wood Brooks, an HBS professor, shared a tool that can help us connect with others. She noted that we often think about six points of separation between us and another person. But what's actually true is that it takes about six questions to find some point of commonality between you and someone else. She noted that not only do questions increase a person's likability and influence, but also, by asking them, you can find a point of relation and connectivity with others.

What my work and research have revealed is that this approach is especially important for you if you're from an underrepresented group in your organization, particularly if you're Black, Indigenous, or a person of color, or in another underrepresented group within your organizational context. This is because affinity bias is at play in the workplace, meaning people are more likely to gravitate to those who are similar to them. Whether a workforce is predominantly white or male or both, or has some other dominant demographic group, when we're in a minority position, affinity biases can work against us. This is because there might be individuals who automatically associate with others who are visibly similar to them. If we're in a minority position, we're more likely to be in a situation where people don't have an affinity for us. While I was writing this book, a study published by Catalyst highlighted that curiosity drives inclusion for people of color at work,[30] and this came as no surprise. The aspects of us that are visible, above the waterline, are only one dimension of our identities, backgrounds, and lived experiences. By asking questions, we can find points of relation that may not initially be visible. If we're from an underrepresented group, we may have to work harder to find that point of connection or affinity, beyond what meets the eye, and questions are the tool to do that.

We'll delve into affinity bias and how to interrupt it later on in this book. When it comes to connectivity, curiosity is an incredibly powerful tool to get to a point of relation and build an affinity with other individuals. As mentioned earlier, there are invisible and visible aspects of you. So think about the visible bits as just the tip of the iceberg, what people see, and underneath are all these other amazing dynamic aspects about you that other people may not see. That's the same truth for others. You want to ask them questions that eventually reveal something about them that may be unknown. Often it takes going beneath the surface to uncover a point of relation, something that you can connect to and build an affinity around. Using questions is an incredibly powerful tool to calm nerves and build points of relation. Go into conversations preparing for what you'd like to know, not just what you want to share.

Use curiosity and questions to focus on the needs of others—and identify the intersection of their needs and your skills. The other powerful aspect of approaching connectivity with a curious mindset is that it will help you concentrate on what you can give. This also helps address the fear that networking is self-serving. Instead of thinking about what you can get, you flip the script and think about what you can contribute.

The more you understand someone else's needs, current situation, context, and challenges, the more you can identify how you can provide value to them through helping solve a problem, sharing expertise, or facilitating a connection. You can't appropriately match your skills and capabilities and resources to their needs without understanding those needs. Asking questions is key to determining what you can give rather than what you can get. Experiment by asking others where they need support or how you can better support them in reaching their goals, what is top of mind for them right now regarding their role or their business, what are the biggest challenges they are facing, what opportunities get them the most excited, or where they see themselves going over the next five years. Picture a Venn diagram with their needs in one circle and your skills, expertise, network, and so forth in the other. By asking these questions, you can push the conversation forward to identify and isolate the area of overlap, the sweet spot where your skills, expertise, and network can help meet the needs of someone else. Making a contribution to others can add meaning to your career, while generating value for others.

Leverage questions to redirect and refocus the conversation. Sometimes despite our best efforts, our conversation partners will put the spotlight squarely on us. At times, this can feel like you're standing at the end of a long hallway with a tennis ball machine launching ball after ball at you so quickly that you're overwhelmed and missing every shot, with no hope of returning the ball in the right direction and putting it in play. When you're on the receiving end of someone firing questions at you, it's helpful to pause and focus on answering one question thoughtfully, finishing with an add-on question that passes the ball back to them. Be prepared with a few talking points and supporting anecdotes about who you are, what you do, why you do what you do, and where you want to go: your goals and aspirations (see chapter 8, "Courageous Advocacy—for You").

Once you've shared an insight, pass the ball back. Imagine being asked about your career aspirations. You could share your desire to be promoted into a role where you have the opportunity to have a bigger impact on your organization and clients. You could then ask your conversation partners what their path to their current position was or whether they have any advice as you navigate this promotion period. Focus on answering one question at a time, even if you miss a few of the balls coming your way, and strategically answer and pass the ball back to them with a question. If your answers and questions can build on known points of relation or commonality with your conversation partner, that's an even bigger win. For instance, "I know you also started in this organization at the associate level. What was your path to management?" In addition to keeping the ball in their court, follow-up questions have also been proven to increase likability and positive perceptions of the conversation. Don't be afraid to use follow-up questions as conversation extenders that allow you to learn more about your partner and connect on a deeper level. Try these: "How so?", "That's interesting. What did you learn?", "I'm interested in knowing more about that. Can you give an example of how this affected your career?", "Wow, that's a tough scenario. How did the situation play out? Where did things land in the end?"

Use curious questioning to move from "small talk" to "deep talk." When you connect with someone new, your natural inclination may be to ask standard small-talk questions like "What do you do?" or "Where are you from?" However, recent research builds a compelling case to use curiosity to go deeper in conversations and, in turn, learn more about others while catalyzing more meaningful and enjoyable conversations. Intimate conversations are correlated with higher levels of happiness in comparison with "small talk."[31] While many of us may steer clear of such conversations with strangers and believe that these more intense conversations are reserved for friends, the studies show that this is misguided and that we probably underestimate how much other people—especially strangers—can enjoy and find satisfaction in more meaningful conversations. In a dozen experiments with roughly 1,800 people, from business executives to visitors in public parks, researchers found that participants felt happier and more connected than they expected after relatively deep conversations with people they had just met.[32]

Try asking deeper questions.

- What do you do? ▶ What do you love doing?
- What is your current role? ▶ What is something about you that is largely unknown, something that isn't in your bio or CV? What is something about you that others may find surprising?
- Where are you from? ▶ Where do you see yourself in five years? What are you most looking forward to in your career over the next year? What's the next thing you'd like to cross off your career bucket list?
- How is your work going? ▶ What aspects of your work do you most enjoy and why? What do you least enjoy and why? What gives you the most meaning, satisfaction, and joy at work?
- How are you? ▶ What's been on your mind recently? What's top of mind for you right now? Is there any type of support you need

right now? What was the highlight of your week? What's been going well? What hasn't been going so well?

Think about adding some interesting questions on risk-taking so that you can learn from others and hear their stories to fuel your practices.

- When was the last time you got out of your comfort zone? How did it go?
- What's the most daring thing you've done in your career?
- What risks are worth taking in life/career?
- When have you failed? What did you learn?

While the evidence strongly suggests swapping "small talk" for "deep talk," the researchers have a word of caution: "Let's be clear. Our research does not suggest throwing all caution to the wind, assuming everyone wants to be your best friend, and revealing your deepest thoughts to anyone you meet. 'Too much information' can be a real thing. Instead, our research suggests that the person next to you would probably be happier talking about their passions and purpose than the weather and 'what's up.'"[33]

Use a curious mindset to move beyond superficialities. Take a try-it-and-tweak-it approach. Try out some questions in conversation, experiment having deeper conversations with new contacts, and then tweak your approach based on how it went.

Leave likability concerns at the door—curiosity has you covered! Networking can be anxiety inducing for anyone, but especially for women who face the added pressure of negotiating the double bind, with research highlighting that women are perceived as competent or liked, but rarely both. To make things more complex, researchers in Canada, Spain, and France studied 221 MBA students who were in their early career years and had six-plus years of work experience, and discovered that women were more likely to define their identities according to how others viewed them.[34] This means that the pressure when networking can seem insurmountable: we must be likable and competent, and the views and judgments of those around us must be positive if we want to form positive identities. That sounds exhausting and anxiety provoking, with an incredible amount of pressure being put on these seemingly all-important interactions.

However, a study published in 2017 in the *Journal of Personality and Social Psychology* provides an easy work-around so that you can simultaneously build deeper, more genuine connections with someone while being more likable: Just ask questions.[35] Yes, it is that simple.

The key finding: People who approach conversations with a curious mindset and ask more questions, particularly follow-up questions, are better liked by their conversation partners and build better connections with more chances for a future connection point.

While this may allay some fears, the women I work with often ruminate for weeks and even months about interactions: fixating on what they should have said, how they could have said it, and what they should have done differently. A team of researchers from Yale, Harvard, Cornell, and the University of Essex found that this negative self-talk and critique is most often biased and overinflated, as "people systematically underestimate how much their conversation partners liked them and enjoyed their company."[36] This "liking gap" is the difference between how much we think people like us and how much people actually like us. Women in particular face this gap. Your solution: Leave likability concerns at the door. Your perception of how much someone likes you is most often going to be skewed, with a glaring gap between reality and what your inner critic is telling you! Use the power of curiosity—asking questions, listening deeply to answers, and asking follow-up questions—to forge meaningful connections while allaying likability concerns.

Getting Past Your Internal Roadblocks

Avoiding networking is a career-limiting and potentially career-stalling move. Don't let the mere thought of networking stop you in your tracks. Use the power of a curious mindset to forge connections while addressing the barriers that may hold you back, including fears, self-doubt, likability concerns, affinity bias, and worries about risks gone wrong.

The most successful women I've met know that no woman is an island and that our connectivity and relationships are critical to our success. They believe that the onus for building and maintaining relationships lies with them and them alone. They proactively and strategically create the meaningful connections they desire through curiosity. Kathleen Taylor, whom you read about earlier in this book, shared: "I am a student of people. One of the things I tell young executives is to build time into their schedules to become students of people and masters of relationships."[37] If you go out with a spirit of curiosity, you'll be amazed at what you can learn about others, about yourself, and about potential connections and intersections, and how you can help others. In the earlier stages of your career, a curious mindset will not only address fears and barriers to networking, but also allow you to tap into the wealth of knowledge of others. Becoming "a student of the people" is a powerful way to unlock learning and catalyze connectivity at this foundational point in your career.

Aspiration-to-Action

Create a comprehensive list of questions you can use in conversations to build connectivity. Understand that some of these questions will be good in some contexts, and other questions in other situations; having an ongoing list is a great starting point. This list can serve as a reference guide as you prepare for connecting with others. You can add to it and revise as you try different questions and approaches.

Some helpful tips:

- Put yourself in their shoes. Remember to think about what you would like to be asked. It makes generating questions easier.

- Search online for helpful tools and tips, especially those from the researchers I mention in this chapter (see the notes for sources).
- Think about what you want to learn. Your early career years are a critical time of learning and development. Think about what you'd like to learn from your conversation partners. Questions about career paths, experiences, key learnings, and advice are great places to start.
- Think about what knowledge you'd like to gain from the other person, in order to better assess how you can be of value to them. You want to be able to find something you can give, not just what you can get. Understanding their needs will help you do this.
- Remember that deeper questions can form deeper connections.

·········· **Risk-Reward-Refine-Repeat** ··········

Risk. Come up with a goal for connecting with others that feels like a stretch or risk for you, something outside your comfort zone. If helpful, you can use the Bold MOVES framework to help you assess which risks to take. What is your Motivation for connecting with someone? What is the Opportunity you have to forge new relationships? What is your Vision if this goes well? Perhaps you make a meaningful connection with someone who can mentor or advise you or someone with whom you can collaborate. What is your Endgame Plan? If things don't work out well, where does that leave you and what will you do? Who is your Support? Is there anyone who can help you prepare for important conversations and opportunities to connect?

My career clients have different fears and risk appetites when it comes to the dreaded networking, which we call "connecting," and so their goals vary. One aimed to attend networking events once or twice a month; she found crowds overwhelming, and we needed to face this head-on. Another client struggled more with video calls and the awkward silences, so we set a goal of connecting with one new person every other week on a call. Another woman set up the goal of reconnecting with two dormant ties every month and one new contact. Another wanted to take a risk and reach out to an executive to ask about a specific need. Create a monthly goal and implement this risk-based goal for three months.

> Complete the sentence: *When it comes to connecting with others outside my comfort zone, the bold moves that I am going to commit to are ...*

Reward. Did you experience any rewards—big or small—from your curious approach to connecting with others? Did your conversations flow differently? Were there different levels of engagement? Did you secure any follow-up discussions or opportunities to continue the conversation? Did you find out someone's needs and how you might be able to help? Did you make any missteps that you learned from? Lessons are also rewards. What was something new that you realized? What was reinforced? Describe the rewards.

Refine. Reflect on how you would refine your approach and method for building and maintaining relationships in the future. What would you do differently? You've tried it, now tweak it.

Repeat. Identify a situation where you will apply these learnings and refined approaches. When is the next time you can use a curious mindset to connect with others? Write it down.

....

CHAPTER 5

Use Curiosity as a Tool of Influence

IT IS A MYTH THAT "GOOD THINGS COME TO THOSE WHO WAIT." The truth: "Good things come to those who ask." However, most of the women I've worked with over the years have shied away from a critically important risk: making the asks that matter.

When women are navigating the inevitable ups and downs of their careers, curious strategic questioning is an underutilized but incredibly effective tool to use in negotiations and challenging conversations. Too often, early career women are told that asking questions will negatively affect them, when in fact questions have the power to build influence and persuasiveness while navigating the gender bind and interrupting bias. If you want to be more persuasive and build influence in any sphere you are in, you can use this chapter to become equipped with the tools to do this, starting from day one in your career.

You cannot get what you do not ask for. That is, if you don't ask, the answer is always no. How you live and work can be determined by whether or not you take the risk to ask for what you want.

In a career context, these asks are the ones that can directly influence your career trajectory, fulfillment, and satisfaction. Whether you are negotiating for a different title, expanded roles and responsibilities, more resources and team support, regular check-ins with a manager, a flexible working arrangement, actionable instead of vague feedback, a promotion, a different compensation package, an ongoing learning opportunity, a sabbatical or leave, or something else, the outcomes of discussions where you make asks have the potential power to limit you or help you learn and grow. Granted, asking for what you want and negotiating for it can be daunting. The key is to learn how to flip the script and perfect what leading organizations, such as BlackRock, have called the Art of the Ask[38] using your curious mindset.

/ **Challenge** / *Women tend to enter challenging conversations armed with defensive tools, which are unfortunately likely to backfire—especially due to gender constructs.*

Research tells us that men often view negotiations and challenging conversation as a game, while women view it more like going to the dentist or having a fight.[39] Unfortunately for women, that means our avoidance tactics are used extensively. Many women report that they would do anything to avoid having a difficult conversation. Others prefer to put up with a negative situation rather than tackle it. If we're preparing for a tough interaction, we know that there's an emotional toll, and we'll start to feel stressed or anxious at the prospect of such a discussion. If we do take the risk to have a challenging discussion or negotiation, we're more likely to spend time preparing what we're going to say than what we're going to ask. We go into battle with full body armor, ready to be on the defensive.

This was the approach I took for many years. I am no stranger to the stage and began public speaking and debating at the age of twelve. I competed in the World Schools Debating Championships three times: in the US, South Africa, and Singapore. After completing my undergraduate degree at Brown University, I went back to the World Championships in Wales, but this time as a judge.

During my university years, I decided I wanted to further develop my communication skills and sought out a class on persuasive communication. After a few sessions, my instructor asked me to come to her office and have a one-on-one. With apprehension and wondering what could be going wrong, I opened the door to her room and took a seat. With a nurturing approach, she said to me: "Christie, how you speak has to counter everything that people will think about you when you walk into a room. This is a common issue for women." She then shared some strategies, including removing filler words, making strong statements rather than asking questions, and ensuring that I didn't have any intonation or upticks in my voice at the end of sentences. I remember thinking that if I lowered my voice and made strong statements, I could increase my credibility and respectability in certain spheres, which was especially important as I sought out summer internships and eventually prepared to enter the workforce after university. I appreciated her candid advice and the actionability of her suggestions, which at the time had reasonable evidence supporting them.

In the years that followed, these techniques shaped my approach to important interactions and presentations. But the techniques I had learned weren't as powerful in practice as I thought they would be. In fact, they even had negative, unintended consequences when it came to negotiations: They backfired. This was a misstep I also saw with my clients as they approached challenging conversations, particularly when the stakes were high.

In my late twenties, after having left Deloitte Consulting and launching my own practice, I was faced with negotiating a long-term contract. I came in with what I thought was a bulletproof proposal, including my other client commitments, demonstrated quality of work, established relationships, credentials, market value, and background. In the end, our discussions reached a standstill, and I realized that a contributing factor was my approach. During my career, I've heard far too many stories of women in the same situation. I learned the hard way that the attributes of a great debater are almost directly the opposite of those of a persuasive negotiator.

It took me years to realize that a debater's approach may not work in my favor or in the favor of those I worked with. Using a debater's strategies, I coached an incredibly smart and gifted woman who was looking for a career transition. After receiving a lowball offer, she resolved to negotiate for her value and worth. In a coaching session, we decided that she should come in with a defensible case with data points and market value, all of the typical negotiation techniques. In the end, the offer that was originally provided to her was rescinded and the overall job offer was withdrawn. The hiring manager relayed that they didn't think her approach or personality would be a good fit for the company. Reading between the lines, it was clear that she had been labeled as aggressive and self-serving for negotiating for her worth, something that happens more to women than to men.

Hannah Riley Bowles, a senior lecturer at Harvard's Kennedy School of Government and codirector of the Women and Public Policy Program, has been studying gender effects on negotiation and "repeatedly found evidence that our implicit gender perceptions mean that the advice that women stand up for themselves and assert their position strongly in negotiations may not have the intended effect. It may even backfire."[40] For my client, the rationale given for rescinding her job offer was not related to her qualifications, background, or experience, but rather to her personality and "fit." These stories are all too common.

As her trusted career adviser, I felt defeated and depleted. I felt that because of her gender, she was unduly penalized for her approach and the risks she took to negotiate. I thought that there must be a better way, so I started researching negotiation techniques and ways to have difficult discussions, then experimenting through trial and error to find what worked and what didn't. I came across one game-changing yet often-underestimated tool: the power of curious, strategic questioning.

/ **Solution** / *Approach challenging negotiations with strategic curiosity, having a point of view but also seeking the advice and input of others and preparing follow-up and probing questions. Spend just as much time focusing on what you're going to ask as on what you're going to say.*

It's hard not to feel helpless or in a bind when we contemplate that there appear to be two options:

1— Take a risk to stand up for ourselves and represent our viewpoints and value with the probable outcome of it backfiring.
2— Stay silent and shy away from difficult discussions and negotiations with the known outcome of maintaining the status quo—including pay, role, and more.

The good news, again, is that there's a powerful work-around you can try in your career. In contrast to what I and many of us were taught, the approaches that we may be told are powerless, such as asking questions or having intonations, are actually incredibly powerful when navigating the gender bind in the workforce. While I admit that there are complexities and nuances here and that the techniques you choose to use and the success of those techniques will be context dependent, I do recommend that you at least try this important tool—a try-it-and-tweak-it approach to experiment with and see what works for you and your career context. When you're preparing for negotiations, curious questioning is also a simple and powerful tool.

In 2013, Adam Grant, author of *Give and Take* and the youngest tenured professor at Wharton, gave a TEDx talk on effective communication techniques. He shared the story of a research project based on team dynamics in a desert island scenario. The group was debating which devices and equipment were essential and which ones were not. The study showed that an individual who said, "The flashlight needs to be rated higher. It is the only reliable night signaling device," was rated as less likable and less persuasive than the person who stated, "Do you think the flashlight should be rated higher? It may be a pretty reliable night signaling device."[41] Framing the same suggestion in a collaborative way through the use of questions increased both likability and persuasiveness. People who framed statements and suggestions as questions have been shown to have more influence in a group and were more successful in securing their suggestions or advocating for their point of view. What wasn't considered in some of these studies was the impact of gender roles and biases. What I have found is that the rewards reaped by using questions are even greater for women, as asking questions dampens the effects of the gender bind. In other words, you can be likable and persuasive! While more work and research on this is required, integrating questions into your difficult conversations is worth trying.

Adam Grant's speech was based on the research of Allison Fragale, a professor and researcher at the University of North Carolina's Kenan-Flagler Business School. Her finding: "An assertive verbal style may enhance your perceived power in an arm's length negotiation, but in collaborative settings, modest speech may win you more support."[42] My finding: This is especially powerful for women, who are expected to be collaborative; if they appear otherwise, they're even less likely to win support and buy-in from others. Curious questioning allows you to be persuasive while navigating the gender bind and learning along the way.

I started to experiment with the use of questions in challenging conversations with some of my clients and then also in my life. What I realized was that framing things artfully as questions, using that spirit of inquiry and a curious mindset in important dialogues, negotiations, and meetings increased the probability of success in getting ideas across, building consensus, having influence, and achieving goals.

Nim, whom you met at the beginning of this book, is one of the most innately curious people I've ever met. She approaches all interactions and aspects of her life with a curious mindset and a voracious appetite for learning. She was the youngest direct report to the CEO of a global organization and was struggling to ignite the change she wanted to have in the organization with her position as manager. She knew she needed a heavier-hitting title to cut through some of the red tape and achieve her goals. She decided to approach the CEO about a change.

She approached her negotiation with a spirit of inquiry. She had a defined intention: That is, she wanted not only to position herself for success in her role but also to drive innovation, experimentation, and connectivity across the company. She had identified the intersection between what she desired and the needs of her boss to attract and retain the brightest and best millennial talent, to be a millennial employer of choice, and to accelerate change and innovation in a family company that was over one hundred and fifty years old. She then harnessed her curiosity to better understand her boss, his needs, and his insights by asking some important questions, including the following: I am grappling with these challenges—what's your advice on how to navigate them? What would you do if you were in my position? How do you envision my role changing and evolving as we set our sights on different priorities and impact? She positioned all of these questions in a compelling way while stressing that the title that she had at present wasn't enough to give her the credibility, authority, and autonomy to achieve the goals to which she and the CEO aspired. She ended the discussion by sharing some potential solutions as options, such as a title change, a way to escalate issues in a timely manner, and greater CEO advocacy. Providing options is another great way to integrate strategic questions into negotiations or discussions. It allows the other person to see a range of options. You pose the questions: What would you prefer? Which option do you think would work best? Options followed by a question is one of the most powerful tools I've seen work in persuasion. In the end, she was successful in negotiating and became the youngest chief officer in the company's history. She leveraged the credibility that came with the title to further push change and ignite innovation in the company.

Adam Grant's TEDx talk featured a similar example in which an early career woman negotiated for travel on a company jet and a stipend for times when the jet wasn't available by using the power of questions. In particular, the question "What would you do if you were in my position?" was shown to increase empathy and to position the person to see something from the other person's point of view and to start to think of solutions for the employee. Katie Liljenquist's research shows that you can "win over an opponent by asking for advice."[43] She provides the example of buying a product: "I love this product and want to buy it, so I'd love your advice on how to make this fit within my budget."[44] Suddenly, that salesperson wants to cut you a break. By asking for advice and insight, you signal to someone that you value their opinion, which is powerful because in order to give you advice, the other person is encouraged to walk in your shoes, to empathize, and to understand your position.

Unlike what I was taught years ago about minimizing questions and upticks, my experiences taught me to consider the reaction someone is likely to have to me. Because we exist in a world with a gender bind, one of the most powerful things we can do is to frame our conversations in a way that leaves room for input from the other person. It's a dialogue infused with strategic and curious questioning and attentive listening, instead of a practiced monologue.

The critical tip here is this: Spend just as much time focusing on what you're going to ask as on what you're going to say. It's important to approach negotiations and important dialogues with a curious mindset and strategic questions, seeking the advice and input of others and preparing follow-up and probing questions.

Put It into Practice

Frame negotiations as opportunities to make an ask. By now, you know that language matters and that the right terminology can help quiet fears and influence action. Similar to the term *networking*, the term *negotiation* can stop the most courageous woman in her tracks. Years ago, when I was facilitating a program for early career women at BlackRock in San Francisco, executives shared the name of their successful negotiation program: the Art of the Ask.[45] As you work through the Aspiration-to-Action section and Risk-Reward-Refine-Repeat exercise of this chapter, stop thinking about negotiating and start framing this as perfecting your art of the ask.

Spend as much time focusing on what you're going to ask as on what you're going to say. In situations where you want to persuade, have influence, build support or buy-in, and make an ask, harness the power of your curious mindset by using strategic questions.

In a recent session I was running for early career women at a leading global investment company, I provided them with a framework to approach challenging conversations, dialogues, negotiations, and other situations where they want to increase their persuasiveness and potential for influence. Based on my work and research and the research of other leaders in the field, including Alison Wood Brooks, Alison Fragale, and Katie Liljenquist, I compiled a quick guide on how to use the power of questions. Some options to try in your own preparations for important conversations are in table 1.

Table 1: Curious Questioning

Ideas	Examples
Ask for advice	I'm really in a bind. I would love your advice. What would you do if you were in my shoes?
Frame your ideas as suggestions — request input and reactions	I wonder if it would work to do it this way? While I understand the hesitation around _____, should we consider the implications of _____ on _____? I was wondering if we're convinced that this is the best we can do, or is there room for improvement?
Position orders as requests or suggestions — frame them as observations followed by a question in need of a response	I noticed _____ and was wondering: Could we try _____? I have been noticing _____. What is the likelihood that we could _____ and when could we start?
Position ideas and solutions as options for input — use the power of "options"	Given the challenges we're facing, I was brainstorming some options on how we could approach this and would like to get your thoughts on what would likely be the best one to try moving forward. Which option do you think would work? Given the current context, which approach of the ones I outlined do you think might work best?
Move from question to clarification — help people transition from providing vague comments and feedback to providing specific and actionable insights	That's interesting. What are the implications? I want to understand this more. Can you give me an example? This is what I heard in our discussion today: [insert summary of what you heard / paraphrase the conversation]. Are we aligned on this? I wanted to confirm that we're all on the same page.

The questions that will work for you will depend on the context and the focus of your conversation. You may be trying to drive a team discussion toward a desired outcome; suggesting a new approach in a meeting; negotiating for a new title or expanded role; providing feedback to a colleague, peer, or junior that you want them to act on; or asking for more actionable feedback from a manager. Across situational contexts, these questions can be customized to help you wield more influence in today's world of work.

When you prepare for discussions and times when you'd like to persuade, ask yourself: What are the questions you want to ask? What do you desire to understand better? What advice or insight would be helpful to you? How could you reframe statements as questions or requests? How can you use the power of questions and providing options together? If you go beyond identifying problems to generating solutions, what questions will you ask an individual or group to get their feedback and insights?

Think about if you were on the receiving end, if you were in the other person's shoes, what questions would you want to be asked?

As Tony Robbins, a *New York Times* best-selling author and coach, says: "Successful people ask better questions, and as a result, they get better answers." Time to ask better questions!

Ignore competency fears and ask powerhouse questions. In a session I ran for a leading global investment company, a woman asked, "How do we do this while still seeming credible? Won't questions make me appear as if I don't have all the answers or the knowledge that I need? I want to ask questions without undermining my competence."

I shared with her a tactic that my coaching clients had used with great success. Hint: It's all about the framing.

We often think that common questions indicate a lack of understanding: "I don't understand. Can you explain?" But we can reframe questions as building on existing knowledge and positioning us for further learning, rather than as just highlighting gaps. More and more companies are seeking critical thinking skills and problem-solvers. By asking insightful questions, you showcase your ability to think critically.

Where credibility concerns are present, or where you're concerned about questions influencing external perceptions of your competence, I want to reassure you that asking questions can actually boost credibility and likability. Research has shown that asking questions can increase both persuasion and influence, confirming that they're not at odds with building credibility and confidence. Instead, questions and credibility go hand in hand.

But, depending on the context, it may not be enough to spontaneously ask a question if there are credibility concerns. So strategic positioning of your questioning can further boost the positive impact of questions. In certain situations, I recommend that women add what I've coined a "competence-building lead-in" to their question.

Instead of saying "Should we consider the implications of _____ on _____?"

Add a competence-building lead-in: "I understand that the current situation is complex given the following factors, including _____. Given these complexities and the hesitation around _____, should we consider the implications of _____ on _____?

Or: "While I understand the core concept here around this engineering model is _____, I am grappling with whether these are the best options for moving forward due to potential unintended consequences. Given _____, can we take some time to consider the implications of _____ on _____?"

The lead-in shows your deep understanding of what's going on and roots your question in the current situation. It also has the added benefit of building a common base of knowledge with the group, summarizing what's going on before you gather reactions.

Imagine a manager was giving you vague feedback—a common challenge for women that holds them and their careers back—and you want to understand his or her viewpoint.

Instead of saying "Can you explain?"

Add a competence-building lead-in: "Thank you for your feedback. While I understand the overall themes you've mentioned, such as _____ and _____, I want to ensure this is actionable. Could you please elaborate on this more? Could we talk through specific examples and then brainstorm actions I can take to address what you've raised?"

Reiterating what you've heard not only conveys understanding of the situation but also ensures that you're on the same page and builds alignment on the situation at hand before you work on a way forward.

Think of the lead-in as a preface to your question that shares your knowledge and showcases what you understand before framing the rest as a question that invites engagement, learning, alignment, and discussion—all while having the potential to increase your influence and persuasiveness.

I assure you that you can project competence, knowledge, and expertise while using questions strategically.

Crush comparisons—they're a futile waste of time and energy. Do men need to think about all these complexities and nuances in communication, persuasion, and influence? In most cases, no. However, in certain situations, where perceived difference is present, such as race, ethnicity, or sexual orientation, they may.

Should society change so that we no longer need to navigate the double bind and can appear likable, competent, and also persuasive without being aggressive? Yes.

But until social attitudes shift radically, and biases are interrupted by new systems and ways of doing work, you as a woman are not immune from these effects. With these tools, however, you can work around them. Remember that the variables involving persuasive communication and negotiations are complex, and you'll need to experiment with these approaches in your contexts to see which ones produce the best results.

Instead of lamenting the extra energy we must put into persuasive communication techniques in comparison with our male peers, let's use that energy to fuel our conversations with strategic questioning and inquiry. In the long run, there are multifactorial wins: wins in persuasiveness, likability, and competence. In addition, you will be able to hone your courageous mindset so that you can continue to grow, learn, and absorb insights and knowledge from those around you as you refine your approaches to work and life. Win, win, win!

An added bonus: You can use these tools and techniques outside the workplace as well. The next time you're faced with a cell phone bill that doesn't seem reasonable, an opportunity to discuss a rental contract, the wrong order at a restaurant, a child who isn't behaving well, or a partner who perhaps isn't sharing the load at home—give these techniques a try. As Maya Tussing, director at BlackRock and developer of the Art of the Ask program, said: "Women who have gone through the Art of the Ask program are asking for things at BlackRock and they are also advocating for themselves at home, for example when they are buying a house. They are saying, 'I am asking all the time and I want to get better.'"[46]

Use Curiosity to Cultivate Risk and Make the Ask

In summary, unleashing your curious mindset to take a risk and make an ask will make you a more influential and persuasive employee, colleague, and leader. By contrast, taking on the risk of negotiation in the absence of curiosity can backfire. My client and I learned that the hard way, but you can begin boldly without facing such consequences. Harness your curious mindset to unlock your power of persuasion while navigating society's pervasive gender bind. It's time to perfect your art of the ask.

Aspiration-to-Action

Brainstorm a list of things you wish you could change in your career. Perhaps you wish you could have more responsibilities in an area that plays to your unique gifts, or work from home one day a week, or receive more support in a certain area. These goals should be realistic. For instance, instead of saying "I wish I didn't have to work Monday through Friday," you could say "I wish I had more control over when and where I worked." Or instead of saying "I wish I never had to do admin," you could say "I wish admin was more equitably shared across the team." Instead of saying "I wish I could be in a leadership role right now," you could say "I wish that I had more opportunities to mentor and lead others in my career context and current role." Instead of saying "I wish I could only do things I enjoy," you could say "I wish I had more time to dedicate to the tasks and roles that give me energy and excitement."

Risk-Reward-Refine-Repeat

Risk. Come up with one ask that's related to one of the items you brainstormed above. It should feel uncomfortable and risky and be something that would enhance your satisfaction and fulfillment in your career. You can use the Bold MOVES model to think through your Motivation for this ask, your Opportunity and opportunity cost, your Vision if you're successful in having your ask met, your Endgame Plan if things don't work out, and your Support system to help you navigate making the ask and any aftermath of making the ask.

Complete the sentence: *The bold move I am going to commit to in my career is making an ask for . . .*

See table 2 for a framework you can use to prepare for your ask. Remember to refer to the content in this chapter to help you compile questions and position options, the bottom two portions of the framework above. Then practice with a partner and go make your ask.

Table 2: Prepare for Influence

Intention	Define Your 'Why' and Begin with the End in Mind • Why is this dialogue important to you? • How do you want them to feel at the end of the conversation? • What do you want them to do? • What is your best-case scenario?
Intersection	Isolate Areas of Shared Interest • Where lies the intersection of interests? • How can you frame the discussions according to this mutual benefit? • How can you help them?
Questions	Ask Questions • What are the questions you want to ask them? • What do you desire to understand better? • What advice or insight from them would be helpful to you? • How can you reframe statements as questions or requests?
Options	Ideate Solutions and Generate Options • What options could you present? • If you were to go beyond identifying the problem to generating solutions, what would your ideas be?

Reward. What were the rewards of making your ask? Remember: Even if you weren't successful in your first try, people generally remember that you made a well-thought-out ask and, when you bring it up again, are more likely to be supportive. This has happened with many of my career clients. Sometimes asks have rewards that are experienced later!

Refine. How did your approach work? What would you refine if you were to try this again? How did this experience and its outcome refine you?

Repeat. When will you make your next ask? What will it be in relation to? Begin to prepare for it now.

....

CHAPTER 6

Harness Curiosity to Optimize Your Time Investment

HAVE YOU EVER FELT PULLED IN TOO MANY DIRECTIONS? Have you ever felt that those in your professional life were being demanding or that no matter what you did your manager wasn't satisfied? Have you ever felt that despite your best efforts, you weren't doing enough? Most of us have been there, and most of us at some point have been told that the solution is better "balance." As a speaker on gender-related issues, I frequently get asked to discuss work-life balance. However, I respectfully decline this topic in favor of a more realistic and empowering approach to "time and energy optimization." While balance is an elusive ideal at best, it also misses an essential point. Instead of imagining a scale with two sides that we're trying to balance, we would be better off imagining a wallet with a limited number of dollars. We have a choice of where to invest those dollars—our time—and we want to invest them in the activities and tasks that produce the most returns. Optimizing our investments means that we have more opportunity to risk intelligently. Not optimizing them will likely result in ongoing feelings of conflict and tension and little energy or time to invest in the chances that matter. What is the rate of return on your investment of time and energy? Hint: If you're investing based on assumptions rather than informed insights, you're likely unintentionally creating a career and life with more tension and less time and energy for risk. Use curiosity to ask, not assume, and optimize your time investment.

/ **Challenge** / *Women struggle to take risks due to competing priorities and feelings of conflict.*

It's easy to feel that you have too much on your plate to leave room for risk or that you already feel stretched, so risking on something important is not even possible. My study revealed that when women are asked why they avoided risk, "competing priorities and commitments in other realms of life" ranks in the top four crucial barriers to risk-taking. When you feel depleted, burned-out, and stretched, your appetite for making bold moves will inevitably decrease.

Before we delve more into this topic, it's important to clarify that this is not a chapter on balancing work and family. Feelings of conflict, tension, burnout, and exhaustion are not reserved for parents alone. Any woman, at any stage of her career, can face these physical, emotional, and psychological burdens. Research shows that the pandemic has only heightened these struggles, and those in the earlier stages of their careers have not been not spared. A study from Indeed found that burnout, a state of emotional and physical exhaustion, is on the rise, and the most-affected populations are Gen Z and millennials.[47] Other studies have highlighted similar trends since the pandemic, with Gen Z-ers the most dissatisfied with current work and life arrangements.[48] Competing priorities, burnout, and feelings of conflict can be experienced by anyone, irrespective of marital or parental status, age, or career level.

If we want to risk intelligently, we must address these feelings of conflict. If balance isn't the answer, what is? The answer is optimization.

/ **Solution** / *Reduce feelings of conflict by using curiosity as a tool to make informed time and energy investments.*

The key to alleviating or reducing feelings of conflict isn't in working harder but in getting smarter around the needs, expectations, and desires of those who matter to you and have a stake in your career and life. In other words, the solution is optimizing your time and energy investments to produce the best returns. The key to optimization: curiosity. While curiosity can't give you more hours in your day, it can help you make the most of those hours so that you can reduce feelings of conflict and free up your time for risk-taking.

When working in consulting, rotating across strategic and people projects in different companies and locations, I realized that the success of most organizations hinges largely on their understanding of the needs of their primary stakeholders, those who have a stake in or influence on the future of their business. These include internal stakeholders, such as employees, leaders, board members, and external stakeholders, such as clients or customers. Leaders seek to understand the expectations of these important people in a structured way, such as stakeholder assessments, customer needs assessments, market assessments, client surveys, and talent and employee surveys and focus groups. All these assessments are based on asking questions to understand the needs and desires of others, ensuring that the business is functioning on data, not assumptions. Despite the fact that understanding expectations is core to the successes of the world's leading organizations, many women don't apply these skill sets to their professional and personal lives; they don't ask.

One of the biggest mistakes that I see women making in the workplace is investing their precious and limited time and energy based on assumption rather than insight. My best bit of advice: Ask, don't assume. It may seem simple, but asking has the power to transform your work and life and to reduce feelings of conflict as you optimize your investments. In short: Use the power of curiosity to optimize your career and life.

Many early career women with whom I work report feeling stretched and burned-out, and this affects their appetite for risk, as risking intelligently takes both time and energy. While we all have twenty-four hours in the day, what can differentiate us is whether we invest that time smartly and in the activities that produce the most returns. I often see women at earlier stages of their careers investing in activities that they think matter at work while overlooking what is actually critically important to their managers and teams. When I say, "Have you asked your manager what matters most to them?

Have you set up time to understand how best to prioritize your tasks according to what is important to your leader?" The answer most often is no. It's easy to fall victim to frantically investing time in things that don't matter, with increased feelings of tension and conflict. I see women receiving negative feedback in performance reviews and delayed promotions because they weren't prioritizing and executing on the things that mattered most to their managers. They were pushing a boulder up a mountain only to reach the top and realize that they were climbing the wrong mountain. They never approached the climb with a spirit of curiosity and never asked their manager for directions on which mountain to climb. I often see women doing this at home as well, investing in things they think matter to their partners and families while not realizing that what really matters is something else. This is poor investment with poor returns.

In her book *Take the Lead*, Betsy Myers speaks about clearly communicating expectations as a core component of life: "Clarity is just as important in personal relationships as it is in business. It is easy to make assumptions about other people's expectations, about what matters to them or what makes them feel appreciated—but again, assumptions can often be wrong. The only reliable way to gain that clarity is to ask."[49] Curiosity leads to clarity. Clarity leads to reduced conflict. Reduced conflict creates more room for risk.

Put It into Practice

Ask, don't assume. So how do we go about doing this? Stew Friedman, an organizational psychologist and the author of *Total Leadership*,[50] suggests that we engage in stakeholder dialogues to verify existing expectations, to change existing expectations where appropriate, and to explore how expectations might be met in new ways. He notes that many people put too much pressure on themselves because they inaccurately inflate the expectations of others and then feel as if they were letting everyone down. Building an understanding of real expectations can alleviate this pressure.

Create a list of your primary stakeholders, your inner circle of relationships, including your manager or team leaders at work, as well as friends and family. Set up time for a structured dialogue with each of them, focusing on what matters most to them. Don't be afraid to ask the important questions. According to Friedman, the goal is to verify and, if necessary, correct your perceptions of expectations. Get clear on what matters most to the people who matter to you and have a stake in your career and life. Curiosity leads to clarity.

Optimize your investments. You've clarified expectations and now you can optimize your investments. If you're investing most of your time at work trying to manage client requests, when what's really important to your manager is executing on a particular project deadline, you can tweak your time investment accordingly. If you're generating stress and conflict in your life by trying to have dinner with your partner or children every evening when what's really important to them is quality time on the weekend when you're less likely to be multitasking and exhausted, then you can tweak your approach. A stakeholder assessment at work and at home allows us to understand expectations and manage those expectations by investing in the activities that mean the most and generate the most value for our stakeholders. We should invest our time for maximum impact and maximum return, rather than investing in things that don't matter to the people we care about and those who have a stake in our careers. I encourage you to set up regular meetings in order to ask questions and pinpoint what matters most to the people who matter, especially in your professional context at work, so that you can always be optimizing your investments. This can be as simple as a weekly meeting with your manager to discuss what was accomplished this week and what you have planned for the next week, asking: "Are these focus areas aligned with your priorities? What matters most to you right now?"

Lead an "outbox life." Betsy Myers encourages individuals to focus on owning their daily decisions. When speaking to a cross-company group of early career women at Baker McKenzie's New York offices, she asked the audience a resonating question: "Are you living an inbox life or an outbox life?" An inbox life is reactive and spontaneous. It lacks structure and involves replying to all items that get sent your way. An outbox life is proactive and focuses on planning, allocating time and energy to identified priorities, and recognizing key areas of influence. Successful women are proactive in their choices, focus areas, and allocation of time. They are the living examples of an outbox life. Inevitably, some part of your day will be spent addressing your incoming requests. But don't lose sight of the balance and don't hesitate to err on the side of strategically investing in crafting an outbox life. Ask yourself: Is the way in which I am spending my time aligned with what matters most to the people who matter to me?

The wallet is in your hands—spend your money wisely. It's time to abandon the elusive quest for balance and focus on the wallet that's in our hands. We get to decide how to spend our funds. We can invest our time and energy dollars wisely, to produce great returns in our career and life, or we can spend on items that ultimately don't matter the most. Using curious questioning to optimize our investments means we have more opportunity to risk intelligently. Not optimizing them results in ongoing feelings of conflict and tension and little energy or time to invest in the chances that matter.

Aspiration-to-Action

Follow Stew Friedman's guidance from *Total Leadership* and create a list of your primary stakeholders inside and outside work. These are the important players in your life, people who have a stake in your future.

Use curiosity to fuel your conversations and create a list of questions you'd like to ask them. The key is to identify what matters most to them.

Capture your findings. What were their top priorities and expectations?

How will you use this new clarity on expectations to optimize how you invest your time and energy? What are you going to do differently? What are you going to prioritize? What are you going to de-prioritize?

Keep yourself accountable for leading an outbox life. Each week, reflect on how much time you have dedicated to what matters most. Does your time allocation match your priorities and what you and others value? If not, what can you tweak to gain greater alignment between what matters and how you invest your time?

Risk-Reward-Refine-Repeat

Risk. Ask yourself: What is a risk that I may have been hesitant to move forward with due to feeling depleted, burned-out, stretched or to having competing priorities? By optimizing my time and energy, how can I move forward to assess this risk (using the Bold MOVES framework) and take it?

> Complete the sentence: *Now that I have minimized feelings of tension and conflict between competing priorities, the bold move I am going to commit to in my career is …*

Reward. Assess your rewards of taking the risk, even if it's lessons learned or new insights on how investing your time and energy based on information rather than assumption has opened new doors for risking.

Refine. How will you refine your approach moving forward? You can also think about how you can continue to use curious questioning to drive the optimization of your investments and leave more room for risk. How can you continue to refine your risk-taking strategies, your outlook, and your investment strategy?

Repeat. Time to repeat. Use your new insights to improve your risk-taking approaches, including how you manage your time and energy to leave room for risk.

PART III

THE COURAGEOUS MINDSET

·········

Imagine you're facing two doors, one labeled *Confidence* and one labeled *Courage*. You can pick only one door to open and should walk through the one that's most likely to set you up for risk-taking and career success. Which one would you pick?

When I did a study and asked women across different stages of their career, "What do you believe is more important in your career and life, confidence or courage?," the overwhelming majority said confidence. This is not surprising: In the rhetoric used when talking about women in the workplace, even in rigorous studies, there has been an immense amount of focus on confidence and not as much on courage. But my work with women over the last fifteen years has shown that the solution to building confidence is focusing not on confidence itself but on unyielding courage.

Confidence is a subjective feeling. It is hard to quantify and is often all-or-nothing. You feel confident, or you don't. You are confident, or you aren't. Confidence can be fleeting. If we're waiting to feel confident before taking a risk, that subjective and elusive feeling may never come, and it may serve as an excuse for playing it safe. But by focusing on courage instead of confidence, we can take bold actions even in the face of self-doubt and fears. In other words, courage can exist in the absence of confidence, and my work has highlighted that focusing on the former can elicit more action and risk-taking!

Confidence is the by-product of courage. By focusing on courageous acts and courageous advocacy, you'll be able to move forward even when you feel the least self-assured. Even in the absence of confidence, even with the presence of self-doubt, courageous acts and courageous advocacy will help you build your courageous mindset and yield confidence as a by-product. Tip: You don't need to feel confident to take risks. You just need to be courageous.

Building a career and life you love takes courage: the courage to claim ownership of your career, pursue risks, persist in the face of setbacks, elevate your voice, and hone your skill sets and mindsets. Taking action requires courage. As Anaïs Nin, a twentieth-century French-Cuban-American diarist and writer, said: "Life shrinks or expands in proportion to one's courage." Your career is no different. Your career shrinks or expands in proportion to your courage. It's time to refocus your efforts from seeking an elusive feeling of confidence to taking decisive action with courage.

....

CHAPTER 7

Courageous Acts

DO YOU KNOW HOW TO SWIM? If yes, think about how you learned. If not, think about how others learned to swim. It's safe to assume that most of us didn't learn by getting pushed off the highest diving board of an Olympic-size pool or pushed off a boat in the middle of the ocean. Most of us started with armbands or flotation devices, in the shallow end of a pool or beach, or at the very least, with a family member or swimming instructor nearby making sure that we kept our head above the water. Over time, we built more courage and faith in our capabilities and skills, and then could take the leap of venturing into the ocean or pool. We started small and then took the plunge. Risk-taking doesn't have to feel like jumping into the ocean when you don't know how to swim. You can start small, build your risk-taking muscle and skill, and then take the leap.

In today's world of instant gratification and public celebrations of big wins and risks taken, early career women too often overestimate the importance of seemingly big choices and milestones, such as deciding whom to work for or getting a big promotion. By contrast, they underestimate the impact of incremental changes and smaller courageous acts, such as speaking up in meetings, raising their hand to take on distinct tasks, using their voice to ask important questions and offer a viewpoint on an issue, setting up standing touch points with a manager, suggesting new ways of doing things, or trying something different in their team environment. These seemingly small acts can cultivate the courageous mindset you need to become a bold and brave risk-taker.

Throughout this book you're encouraged (even the word *encouraged* has courage at its core!) and equipped with the tools to take risks. This topic isn't limited to this chapter alone. However, this chapter will help you understand the power of everyday "micro-acts of courage" and put them into practice. Think about these micro-acts as learning how to tread water before taking a bigger plunge. Hint: Don't underestimate the importance of small courageous acts or overestimate the impact of big ones. Courage begets courage. It's a muscle that gets stronger each time you use it, no matter how small the act. Time to flex your courageous mindset muscle by starting with micro-acts of courage.

/ **Challenge** / *Until they feel confident, women have a tendency to avoid pursuing stretch goals and opportunities.*

Have you ever shied away from taking on a role or opportunity because you didn't feel confident enough? Perhaps your inner critic told you that you weren't yet ready, weren't capable enough, or didn't have enough experience. Perhaps the voice in your head asked: "Why me?" If you can relate, you're among the majority of women with whom I have worked. During my most recent study, I asked: If you have ever avoided risks, what factors and reasons contributed to this? Over 70 percent reported that self-doubt—not believing in themselves, their capabilities, and their skills—was a driving factor.

This information shouldn't come as a surprise. We know self-doubt is a pervasive and often-paralyzing concern, particularly for women. A thorough study by a Cornell psychologist and a Washington State psychologist highlighted higher levels of self-doubt in women,[51] and years later the famous Hewlett-Packard study showed that women will apply for a job only if they meet 100 percent of the qualifications, while men will apply when they fulfill only 60 percent.[52] Ultimately, men take more chances on themselves, and that pays dividends in the long run.

When we look closer at the data, not taking risks due to self-doubt boils down to a lack of confidence accompanied by a fear of failure and rejection.

As Katty Kay and Claire Shipman reinforced in their *Atlantic* article: "Compared with men, women don't consider themselves as ready for promotions, they predict they'll do worse on tests, and they generally underestimate their abilities."[53] Other studies highlight that women are more likely to underestimate their capabilities and strengths, viewing themselves as less skilled and less talented than others would report. A recent study found that there's a substantial gender gap, with women systematically providing less favorable assessments of their own past performance and potential future ability than equally performing men, with men having rated their performance 33 percent higher than equally performing women.[54] In regard to self-evaluation, women systematically provided less favorable assessments of their performance and potential future ability than equally performing men. Lack of confidence in their abilities skews self-assessments for women and perceptions of readiness and capability, affecting propensity for and willingness to risk.

/ Solution / *Focus on courage over confidence.*

What's one of the biggest areas of challenge for early career women? This is the question my research partner, Lauren Noël, and I asked top business executives from some of the world's leading companies. The resounding answer: confidence.

Notwithstanding this perception, many of the most successful senior women leaders we interviewed about their own career journeys didn't embody confidence when sharing their stories or talking about their skills. This contrasted with executives who were pointing to closing the confidence gap in women as the solution to long-term career success. But successful senior-level women leaders themselves were self-reporting that they had been successful and built vibrant and fulfilling careers even with self-doubt and lack of self-esteem. There was a disconnect. How could they have been so successful? If they were still lacking confidence, how had they built meaningful and dynamic careers in which they thrive? The answer: courage.

Women across ages, levels, and stages of their careers undermine their own strengths and grapple with self-doubt or the extensively studied *imposter syndrome*, the persistent inability to believe that success is deserved or has been legitimately achieved as a result of effort or skill. When Lauren and I were conducting interviews, we often were taken aback when successful and inspiring women we interviewed, including global leaders of worldwide organizations, would start off an interview by saying that they were unsure if they had anything interesting to share, were questioning how they had been chosen to be featured, and noted that it was fine if their comments ended up being edited out of articles. We noted that women understating their accomplishments and unique gifts occurred irrespective of position or level of success.

Once we delved into the interviews, these same women proceeded to blow us away with their inspiring accounts of failures, triumphs, and resilience. They shared amazing stories of moving across the world and taking on new responsibilities and roles; of rising to the occasion when faced with the difficult trade-offs between work and family; of dealing with loss, grief, and failure; and most important, of taking risks. These women were dynamic, brave, and fascinating individuals. What they had in common was courage in the absence of confidence. Amazing women who have been the most successful by any reasonable internal or external measure don't show up confidently every day, but they do show up courageously every single day. Standing in front of a room of early career women at a conference in Toronto, one executive was asked how often she feels afraid. She said, "Every day," and encouraged everyone in the room to do something that scared them every day.

When working with early career women, I have found an overwhelming number of them reporting: "But I'm not confident enough." The stories of female executives and trailblazers show us that to take smart risks, we should repurpose the time we spend thinking about needing more confidence and instead focus on building more courage through action. Remember: You don't need to have confidence to be courageous. But you can be courageous in the absence of confidence, and confidence can actually be a by-product or output.

Stop seeking an elusive feeling of confidence, often fleeting, something that may leave us when we mess up or we fail, and instead think about "How can I be courageous? How can I focus on courageous acts, no matter how seemingly small?" That leader speaking to the room of early career women gave some great advice. You should do something outside your comfort zone every single day.

Choose courage over confidence. You can't learn to swim by standing on the shore and waiting to feel confident. You need to have the courage to get in the water before you feel confident and build your swimming skills.

Put It into Practice

Don't underestimate the impact of small yet significant acts of courage or overestimate the impact of seemingly large ones. Very few early career women with whom I've worked realize the power of what I call "micro-acts of courage"—seemingly small-scale acts that have incremental impacts over time and long-term returns. These micro-acts are the key to unlocking your courageous mindset and realizing the power of risk in your own career and life. Offering a viewpoint in a meeting may seem insignificant in isolation, however, over time, offering ideas and solutions in meetings can differentiate you as someone who has valuable input and insights. In addition, you'll cultivate your courageous mindset and prepare yourself for bigger and bolder moves, such as presenting in front of leadership or clients or key stakeholders or investors. Small acts of courage can then be scaled! Su-Mei Thompson, CEO of Media Trust, shared: "It is not just about taking a few big risks but about pushing yourself each day to get outside of your comfort zone."[55]

Leena Nair used this approach when focusing on using the power of her voice and being heard in meetings. She used her courageous mindset and spoke up in meetings early on in her career when she was one of the few women in the room. "I used to have a little book in which every time I spoke up, I would draw a star. If I opened my mouth five times, then I would draw five stars. If I made a point that really resonated, I gave myself double stars. By doing this, I kept myself accountable."[56] Micro-acts of courage led to long-term rewards. As chief HR officer at Unilever, she achieved many firsts: the first female, first Asian, and youngest ever CHRO of Unilever. Small acts of courage helped her achieve amazing wins that have now led to her role as CEO of Chanel.

Leena Nair's lessons on small acts with big returns can help early career women get past their fears of risk-taking. A coaching client of mine was struggling to get comfortable with risk-taking. We worked on micro-acts of courage every week and touched base to look at the improvements. In six months, she went from not speaking in meetings, even when called on, to proactively planning agendas for meetings, offering viewpoints, and helping devise a plan for more structured and effective meetings. The most meaningful change was the result of one small courageous act: setting up structured weekly touch points with her manager. Initially, she was nervous about taking time on someone's calendar, about being an inconvenience, about appearing like she was just trying to promote herself. But she took the leap because it felt like a smaller act of courage. She progressed from not sharing her weekly progress and plans to having weekly times set up with her manager to share what she had worked on, what she had accomplished, and what she had planned. By the end of our time together, she had been offered an expanded global role. The time with her manager gave her an opportunity to showcase her progress, align on priorities, ask critical questions, and keep and share a track record. This served as a great reference for performance reviews and discussions down the line. In her review of our time together, she shared: "Working with Christie has helped me take on small, manageable, and meaningful tasks each week to help with discrete improvements." Those small, manageable, and meaningful tasks were micro-acts of courage. Those discrete improvements added up. This is the surprising power of small acts of courage.

Practice courageous acts in other spheres of your life. If you struggle to take risks in your career, taking courageous actions outside of work may be a good place to start. One woman with whom I worked at an earlier stage in my career made a goal of going on a dinner or date or lunch with someone new every week so that she could expand her friendships and dating prospects in a new city while becoming more connected. Others will go out of their comfort zone and join a gym or fitness class that they previously would have shied away from. Others started saying no more often, protecting time for themselves, rather than trying to please others. Each year, Leena Nair sets a goal for herself to learn something new. In the past, she has learned how to play an instrument and has signed up for a digital class. One thing that she has repeatedly tried to learn but cannot is driving. She recalls, "Every three or four years, I say 'I have to master this driving thing' but I fail. I want to show my children that I can fail badly at something and still succeed," she explains. Her sons' response? "They say, 'Don't make a life philosophy out of everything, Mom. It's okay. You can't drive.'"[57] The powerful lesson here is that we can take courageous action outside work, in small but meaningful ways.

Making connections when you're shy or hesitant, joining a gym or class outside your comfort zone, learning how to say no and set boundaries, learning a new skill or language outside your area of expertise: All of these small courageous acts can transform your life when you commit to doing them consistently. Nervous to start in your working environment? Start with courageous acts outside work. You'll develop your courageous mindset so that you can use it effectively in your career. It's a transferable mindset that then permeates all aspects of your life. In fact, a courageous mindset is a precondition of success in all areas of our existence. You have to cultivate it through action. Let's build yours.

Try Again Tomorrow

Courageous acts should be continuous—a daily commitment to going beyond your comfort zone. Dr. Elizabeth O'Day founded Olaris, Inc., a precision diagnostics company working to change how diseases are treated. Now in her midthirties, she serves as the company's CEO, cochair of the World Economic Forum's Global Future Council on Biotechnology, and a member of *Scientific American*'s Steering

Committee for the publication's "Top 10 Emerging Technologies." Her impressive résumé doesn't tell the full story of the challenges she has overcome.

"Every day as a young female scientist CEO in biotech, there are challenges, and it takes a lot of courage to face these challenges," she said. "I often remember the quote by Mary Anne Radmacher, 'Courage does not always roar. Sometimes courage is the quiet voice at the end of the day saying, I will try again tomorrow.'"

Aspiration-to-Action

Brainstorm a list of small courageous acts, micro-acts of courage, that you could take in your career. These are conscious and courageous acts in situations that feel risky, uncertain, or ambiguous. For example, these could include the following:

- Challenging yourself to speak up first in small groups
- Putting yourself up for consideration for supporting a small project or initiative
- Setting up a weekly touch point with your manager
- Making a cold call or offering to reach out to someone your team doesn't know
- Offering to take the first stab at a proposal or presentation
- Sharing a viewpoint in a meeting that could be controversial

·················· **Risk-Reward-Refine-Repeat** ··················

Risk. Come up with one small courageous act that feels risky and outside your comfort zone.

Complete the sentence: *The courageous act I am going to commit to over the next month is...*

Reward. Remember that real and meaningful progress is often slow and incremental. Through the Risk-Reward-Refine-Repeat model related to courageous acts, you can cultivate a culture of continuous improvement in yourself. What are the small wins you can celebrate? Remember not to diminish the powerful impact of micro-acts of courage done consistently over time!

Refine. Consistently track your own progress. For instance, keep tabs on how many times you speak up, offer a viewpoint, compile an important communication, or take action outside your comfort zone. Being aware of your own benchmarks will allow you to see improvements over time. Capture what's working and what isn't. How will you refine your approach moving forward?

Repeat. Building your courageous mindset requires intentional and ongoing repetition. What courageous acts can you continue to repeat in your career context? These will help you hone your ability to take bigger risks in the long run.

....

CHAPTER 8

Courageous Advocacy—for You

HAVE YOU EVER SHIED AWAY FROM SHARING YOUR CONTRIBUTIONS, your experience and qualifications, or your accomplishments? Even in the most supportive of settings, it can feel difficult to talk about ourselves. However, advocating for yourself is critical to being a successful risk-taker. If people are aware of who you are, why you do what you do, your impact, your value, and your aspirations, you will be better positioned to take risks successfully and build your powerful $\underline{S}$upport network (the S in Bold MOVES).

As you learned in the preface, I was a prime example of someone who shied away from self-advocacy. Like many women with whom I've worked, I grew up thinking I could keep my head down and do good work and it would eventually be recognized. The reality is that your work can't be recognized if people don't know about it. In my twenties, my career counselor at my organization told me: "You are lucky other people are tooting your horn for you. But at some stage, you need to be able to do the same for yourself." Like many women, I loved cheerleading for others but fell short when it came to myself. Although the image of me tooting a horn wasn't enticing, her message that I needed to better represent myself stuck with me. Through self-advocacy you can build awareness of your story, your work, your why, your impact, and more, while addressing gender-specific challenges to fulfilling your career aspirations and setting yourself up to take risks.

/ **Challenge** / *Contrary to popular belief, the workplace is not a meritocracy. Talent and hard work alone will not get you ahead.*

As women, we tend to believe that our good work should speak for itself—that we shouldn't need to promote it or make it obvious to others. But one only needs to look at numerous research studies over the last twenty years, the lack of women in leadership positions, or class-action lawsuits on gender bias in pay and promotion to realize that this is not the case. As Lois P. Frankel, a psychologist and the author of the best-selling book *Nice Girls Don't Get the Corner Office*, warns: "Hard work typically begets more hard work."[58]

What Lauren Noël and I discovered through our studies on early career and senior-level women is that women enter the workforce believing that it's a meritocracy and that hard work alone will get them recognized, but after years of experience they realize that the obstacles they face are different from those of their male peers. *Real talk*, also known as facing the facts and not glossing over the current state of play in the world of work, is required earlier to ensure women make the most of their early career years and opportunities with eyes wide open! The sooner we know about obstacles and barriers to progress and satisfaction, the sooner we can find ways to address them.

Women can shy away from things that appear self-serving and also err on the side of giving credit to teamwork instead of individual contributions. Do any of these statements or sentiments sound familiar?

- "I will just keep my head down and do the work. It will pay off in the long run. My work will speak for itself."
- "Self-promotion feels icky and forced. It's self-serving."
- "I'm lucky. I've never needed to toot my own horn. I've been fortunate enough to have good opportunities come my way."
- "I don't want to play this game."
- "I don't like talking about myself."
- "I want to talk about my team and their efforts. That's the most important thing."

- "The workplace seems fair. I've never been subjected to bias."
- "I don't want to come off as arrogant."
- "I've heard about the double bind. If I self-promote, I may be viewed as more competent but less likable. It isn't worth the risk."

The harsh reality: Doing a good job is not enough. You might have a boss who has never promoted a woman or who doesn't believe women can juggle work and home. You might face gender stereotypes and unconscious bias and be viewed differently than your male peers. You may receive extra scrutiny in comparison with your equally qualified male counterparts, and this issue may be amplified during your early career years when the lack of a track record leaves you more vulnerable to people's subjective opinions rather than objective criteria. These and many more obstacles can put the brakes on your career aspirations. However, not all hope is lost! Here's what you need to know and what you can do to advocate for yourself.

/ **Solution** / *Be your own best advocate. Craft and control your narrative.*

First, let's acknowledge a gender complexity here: Yes, women who *self-promote*, meaning, promote or publicize oneself or one's activities, get treated differently than men who do. But this is not a reason to avoid it. Research from Catalyst asked: What works best for women? One career strategy stood out as having the greatest impact. Women who did more to make their achievements known advanced further, were more satisfied with their careers, and had greater compensation growth.[59] In short: Self-advocacy is worth the risk! You just need to be skillful and strategic when doing it.

First, it's up to you to craft, control, and share your own story: your narrative. The alternative is someone else telling it for you on their terms, with their own interpretations and assumptions. How you approach this is important. Over ten years ago, I developed a session for women at a Big 4 consulting firm titled "Tooting Your Own Horn." This company and others recognized the self-promotion gender gap and were actively trying to equip women to better advocate for themselves. I went on to run other client sessions like "Self-Promotion" and "Practicing Your Elevator Pitch." What I realized throughout years of presentations on similar topics is that the framing matters, and again, the language we use matters.

With a photo of a woman holding up a gigantic horn on the screen, I saw the participants sink back into their chairs at even the thought of "tooting their own horn." I similarly saw women shy away when told they had thirty to sixty seconds in an elevator to tell someone about themselves, and I also learned through research and practice that rushed monologues are never as productive or persuasive as using a curious mindset and making it a collaborative and inquisitive dialogue. I also felt that these scenarios were forced: When was the last time you had a protected thirty to sixty seconds of someone's time in an elevator alone? And women generally expressed discomfort with the word *promotion* which for them generated comparisons to being a product or item or brand to promote, rather than a person with human complexities and a story. The solution to all of these barriers and the resistance and discomfort related to terminology is simply to reframe. What we are working on in this book is your *narrative*, taking ownership of your journey and crafting your own personal story. It is this language and framing that allows you to produce your best insights and move past internal resistance and setbacks.

Claudia F. Prado, who sat on Baker McKenzie's Global Executive Committee and was the former chair of the Global Diversity and Inclusion Committee, has advice for early career women: "Get out of the passenger's seat and into the driver's seat of your career."[60] One of the most important aspects of driving is crafting and controlling your own story.

Many of the women I have worked with have faced almost paralyzing angst and distress during a career transition or break.

- What will people think of me?
- When and how should I update my LinkedIn? (This lingering question has kept many up at night!)

- I'm shying away from networking events and going out because I don't know how to explain myself and am fearful of people asking me questions.
- I don't even know who I am anymore or how to present myself.

One of my clients was a young executive at a global company. When leadership changed, the scope of her role and autonomy to set strategies and execute effectively were reduced. With a lesser role and changed reporting structure, she decided to leave the company without another role lined up. Deflated and depleted by the experience, she struggled to accurately reflect her narrative in conversations and missed critical opportunities to share her powerful story and reasons for her transition. She didn't know how to represent herself without a current job title. At networking events when people asked what she did, she nervously laughed and said she was "funemployed," meaning she was unemployed and just having fun. But this one word didn't do her or her story justice. She could have shared what her prior role was, the astounding impact she created on the organization, the legacy of programs she left the organization with, her reasons for transitioning out, and her aspirations for the future.

Another close connection of mine made the bold move of leaving her HR role at a prominent professional services firm to pursue her long-standing passion for arts and museum studies. She was studying for her master's degree in museum studies at Harvard Extension School while volunteering at multiple local charities focused on historical preservation, and working part-time for a national museum. When people asked her what she was doing, she said: "I'm taking a career break," when she clearly was strategically career building. These women and many others didn't do justice to their dynamic journeys. Don't undersell your story. And don't leave yourself up to interpretation.

Craft and trial your own personal narrative—a story that's uniquely and authentically yours, grounded in your Who, What, Why, How, and Where. Here's a simple but impactful template (table 3) I've used with thousands of women across the globe.

Table 3: Crafting and Controlling Your Narrative

WHO you are	What do you want people to remember about you? What's unique about you? *Tip:* If you're struggling to answer this, harness the insights of others in your close circles to help you. Sometimes you can't see yourself clearly until you see yourself through the eyes of others. Pick five to ten close contacts and ask them: What are my unique differentiators? What makes me uniquely me? What are the special aspects of me that set me apart? What is my special edge? Who am I when I am at my best? Look for themes and then think about how you'll integrate these themes into your narrative, ideally with supporting anecdotes.
WHAT you do	What do you do? *Tips:* This can be framed as more than a title or role or organization. Instead, think about it as your function. This is what you actually do, instead of how you are labeled! Frame it as a question or topic related to the problems you help others solve. "Do you ever struggle with making time for strategic projects in your role, while dealing with day-to-day competing priorities and deadlines? As strategic project support, I ensure leaders and organizations are able to execute on their important priorities and projects, no matter what else is going on." "Now more than ever, Diversity and Inclusion is a need to have, no longer a nice to have. I champion these efforts and ensure we are moving toward action and the results that matter to our people."
WHY you do what you do	Why do you do what you do (demonstrate your passion)? Why is what you do important? What problems are you seeking to solve for others? *Tip:* Remember the great quote from Simon Sinek, British American author and inspirational speaker: "People don't buy what you do, they buy why you do it." What's your 'why'? Make your narrative more compelling by honing in on your 'why' and articulating it.

Table 3: Crafting and Controlling Your Narrative *continued*

HOW you deliver value / make an impact	How do you make an impact? What contributions have you made to the teams, organizations, and communities you're a part of? *Tip:* Here's a great place to highlight measurable results! More on that to follow, but this is particularly important for women.
WHERE do you want to go	Where do you want to go from here? What are your goals and aspirations? *Tip:* Describe your immediate goals. These should be concrete and well defined.

Remember that unlike the outdated elevator pitch exercise, this doesn't need to be something you're expected to reel out quickly under a tight time frame. The goal is to crystallize these aspects of you for yourself and then use them strategically in discussions with others to represent you and your value.

Before we put this into practice, one word of caution. The language you use to talk about yourself matters. The most common pitfalls that I see women make include the following:

- Talking about activities, instead of impact.
- Using passive and powerless words, instead of active and powerful words.
- Talking about personal characteristics, instead of results.
- Using the language of "we" and not balancing it with the language of "I."

Why do these pitfalls need to be called out and addressed? In 2015 I attended a session in Boston led by the Clayman Institute for Gender Research at Stanford University. The presentation featured a summary of research from their institute and others over the years that showed that in comparison with your male peers, you will:

- Receive more scrutiny, including doubt-generating statements. For instance, someone might say they would need to see more proof of your efforts to put you up for a promotion or to support a role change for you.[61]
- Have criteria enforced more rigidly or change unexpectedly. For instance, criteria for being hired, promoted, and so on.[62]
- Have people talk about your appearance and personality more.[63]
- Be described by others with softer, communal language, the language of "we," that is, using terms such as collaborative and helpful, a team player, which unfortunately makes you less likely to appear as a "fit" for leadership roles.[64]

The way to address this is to take the following actions.

Highlight impact, not just activities. Transition from focusing on what you're "doing" to what "value" you've generated and what "impact" you've had. When you were a college student, did you organize any events that were successful? If yes, how many people attended and what was the feedback? Did you have a student leadership role? If yes, what did you accomplish during your time in the position? Did you help your organization increase sales? If so, by how much? Did you contribute to building or enhancing a campaign, product, or service? Did you lead the development of any internal initiatives that benefited the company and its employees? How have you made an impact on your company, your team, your clients, your markets, and the brand? Depending on your career stage, you can think about examples from university or college, internships, summer jobs, volunteer roles, and your current position. For instance: "I managed an event." Great time to insert an example with results! "In my final year of college, I led a diverse group of students, from different years, majors, demographic groups, and more, in organizing the most well-attended virtual student forum that the school had ever seen. The feedback has been amazing, and now that I have left, the students who were involved are using our process as a template for future events. It's been rewarding to see how connecting with a dynamic group of people for a distinct event can have a long-term impact on how events are organized and run on campus." See other reframing examples in table 4.

Table 4: Activities vs. Impact

Activities	Impact
What you have done	**What you have accomplished**
Managed client relationships	Managed x client relationships across y (e.g., accounts / industries / departments / length of time) resulting in z (e.g., referrals, sales, revenue, cost reduction).
Organized a student event	Organized an event, including x volunteers across student groups. Brought together y attendees, and raised z dollars for an important cause.
Managed the company's social media platform	Increased our following by x accounts and our profile visits by y.

Team up with someone—a coach, mentor, *Begin Boldly* accountability advocate, or peer—to identify your measurable contributions to your teams, clients, and organization. Early in your career this may seem daunting, but your impact doesn't depend on tenure or seniority. It happens from day one and should be brought to the forefront of discussions. It could be from helping develop a client presentation that sells a new product, or working on a proposal that secures new business, or contributing to a marketing campaign that does well, or developing a new product idea. You aren't just a doer. You generate value. Speak to that and remember to integrate your impact into your résumés, cover letters, and online narratives.

Choose active language rather than passive and powerless words. When rereading résumés, profiles, and narratives, I frequently guide the women I work with by saying "I want every bullet you write to start off with a powerful action verb." One woman shared with me that she "traveled" to a conference, but when I probed with questions, I discovered that she played a critical role in organizing it. Another woman noted that she was "invited" to attend a global meeting. Again, after being questioned, she revealed that she actually presented at an executive board session. When in doubt, look at a word and ask: What did I actually do? Is this captured here? Review your narrative with that lens and look to integrate more powerful action verbs (see table 5) to capture the essence of your activities and contributions.

Table 5: From Powerless to Powerful

More Passive / Powerless	More Active / Powerful
Engaged in	Drove the development of
Attended	Spearheaded
Traveled to	Led
Was invited to	Cultivated
Sat on (the committee or board)	Advised
	Worked on
	Initiated
	Liaised with
	Managed/Organized

Emphasize results, not just personal characteristics. Are you someone who is a people person? Perhaps you're very organized or a great leader? Maybe you're someone who is dedicated to always improving and growing? Don't just describe yourself with words, showcase your results. For instance: "I am someone who is dedicated to always improving and growing." Great time to insert an example with results! "I have proactively sought out ongoing learning opportunities and recently completed a professional certification program. In addition, through focusing on my development plan at the company, I have been able to improve my rating on a critical competency area for my role. I am proud of my measurable progress and results and look forward to continuing my growth." The difference between speaking to impact and speaking to results? Your impact relates to the effect of your actions on your clients, team, organization, and others around you. Results relate to showcasing progress and outcomes that may be on an individual level. Women are often described by their personality traits, while men are described by accomplishments. It's time to level the playing field by making a conscious decision to speak to results over characteristics. Tip: Encourage those who mentor, manage, and support you to do the same in your performance reviews, evaluations, recommendation letters, and references.

Integrate some "I" language to balance out "we" language. Research from the Stanford's Clayman Institute for Gender Research highlights that the language of "I," termed *agentic* language, is associated with leadership.[65] One study showed that two applications for a position were submitted with the same qualifications but using different language. The applicant with the more communal language, the language of "we," was less likely to be offered the job. Examples of words associated with "I" are *intellectual, confident, influential, determined, direct, driven*. Examples of "we" words are *helpful, supportive, team player, friendly*, and *collaborative*. I'm not suggesting that you should not use the "we" words if they accurately describe your traits. Instead, what I'm proposing is that if you possess traits associated with "I," you should look at integrating "I" words into your narrative and how you talk about yourself. There's power in collaboration and supportiveness and an overall communal approach to work. However, a balance of language that represents you authentically is your best card to play, given that studies show that women don't use "I" words enough to describe themselves or other women. Language matters! Let's translate these insights into action.

Put It into Practice

Own your story, don't defer that power to others. This isn't a pitch or a promotion. It's simply you taking control of your story, getting in the driver's seat of your narrative, and sharing it. It's about being your own best advocate rather than leaving yourself up to interpretation. Your story is yours to craft. Empowering? Yes. You are the storyteller of your life. Write it and share it on your own terms.

Remember that you are more than your job, your role, or your title. Your narrative should reflect this. Resist the temptation to refer to those descriptors alone. Don't diminish yourself or oversimplify yourself by tying your identity to a singular title or organization. You are dynamic and multidimensional. Represent these interesting aspects as you describe yourself. Additionally, the world is uncertain. If anything, COVID-19 has shown us that. If you lose your job, if you are made redundant, or if you decide to move, you want an identity or narrative that can move and evolve with you and isn't tied to one role. I've seen too many women struggle with identity crises when they leave a role, decide to take time off, or stop playing a sport that has defined them. You are not one dimensional. Your identity is dynamic (see chapter 11, "Agile Identity"). Own that and represent it, rather than running the risk of investing too much emotional attachment to one aspect of your identity.

Don't be afraid to share big and bold goals. When I was in college, one of my professors and a longtime mentor, the late Josef Mittlemann, encouraged our class to use Jim Collins's BHAG (pronounced "bee hag") model in our own lives. Originally designed for companies, a BHAG is a "Big Hairy Audacious Goal" that, when crystallized and shared, is a powerful way to stimulate progress. On an individual level, a BHAG serves as a clear and compelling objective that builds accountability; once we share it, it becomes a reality for us, as well as building momentum toward achieving it. Too often women shy away from sharing big goals because of self-doubt (What if I fail or don't achieve this?) or concern for others' perceptions (What if I come off sounding too ambitious and aggressive?). However, the impact of sharing a goal is immeasurable, and the benefits far outweigh the concerns. You hold yourself accountable and create the opportunity for others to hold you to account as well. You speak it into existence—it becomes an undeniable reality for you once you get it out of your headspace and into airspace. You increase the probability of success as those around you can be aware and contribute to your reaching your goals by identifying opportunities and connections for you that may help. Leena Nair emphasized the importance of identifying and articulating your ambitions to others. She talked about becoming the CHRO for Unilever eight years before she assumed the position. "Put your dreams out there. Be vocal about the way you think. One of the things that holds women back is their perceived lack of ambition. They fear standing up there and expressing themselves. Ambition inspires people. It takes courage. Face the fear and say your big dream out loud."[66] To advance your career, it's vital to set goals and have conversations about what you hope to achieve. Don't just think "I should get a promotion or take this opportunity." Pursue those conversations and be an active driver of your own destiny. Sharing your goals will help you identify risks worth taking that are associated with those goals and build your *S* in Bold MOVES, your Support network of people who are aware of your goals.

Share supporting stories and anecdotes. Stories make words come to life. As a former recruiter, Human Capital consultant, and an interviewer and selector for the Rhodes Scholarship, I have learned that anecdotes outweigh words. If you say something, think of a corresponding example that would demonstrate this. Stories help bolster your narrative by making it come to life and making it more memorable. When you describe how you deliver value, share a story to demonstrate this. Instead of just saying, "I deliver value to my organization by being a connector of people and opportunities," you can add, "For instance, I've been able to identify four new client accounts through having conversations with targets about their needs and matching them to the appropriate service." An example of someone with a compelling story is Maggie Georgieva from Bulgaria, who, at the time of our interview, was a deeply talented product manager at HubSpot, a high-growth inbound marketing firm headquartered in

Cambridge, Massachusetts. Lauren Noël and I interviewed Maggie for our report "What Executives Need to Know about Early Career Women." Maggie shared her 'why': she's "passionate about the changing landscape of marketing and new media technologies," and her 'how': "she takes risks and learns quickly."[67] However, it's her story that makes her come to life: Maggie joined HubSpot after graduation and months later set the Guinness record for designing and delivering the world's largest marketing webinar. Measurable, impactful, and memorable! Since our interview, she's progressed to group project leader. You may not have as grand of a story to share (yet!), but keep an ongoing log of stories and anecdotes that support your narrative. Do this throughout the year so that when those annual self-evaluations come up, all the data is there, ready to be sculpted into a compelling evaluation. Reminder: This links nicely with prior points on highlighting impact and results. Stories and anecdotes are a great way to do this.

Look for opportunities to integrate your narrative into a range of discussions and platforms. Update your LinkedIn, résumé, and social media platforms. Share aspects of your story in conversations, cover letters, and interviews. Integrate parts of your story, such as your What or How or Where, into your performance reviews and career discussions. Link them with the common thread of your narrative.

Examine and enhance your language. The language that you use to talk about yourself matters. Remember to talk about impact, use active words, highlight results, and integrate some "I" language.

Continue to build on your story as you grow. Let your narrative grow with you. Remember that this is a living, breathing, and ever-evolving document. As you change, so does your narrative. Right now, you're laying the bricks and mortar foundation, but over time you'll be building a much bigger and more dynamic structure. Each brick is an aspect of your story, a piece that comes together to make the masterpiece of your narrative.

Get in the Driver's Seat: Shape Your Story

By crafting and controlling your narrative, you have an opportunity to make others aware of what you're working on, what matters to you, and where you aspire to go and grow! It makes your achievements visible, your work and ideas accessible, and showcases that you believe in your value and worth. You have the tools to shape your reputation and to influence what you're known for. Crafting and controlling your story will put you in a better position to take on risks and prepare for outcomes.

During your early career years, you may be particularly hesitant to call attention to your work and progress. This is your time to get your bearings, adjust to the world of work, and try to figure things out before you start to call attention to your contributions ... right? Wrong! This is a critical time to quiet your inner critic and advocate for yourself and others. Don't get taken for a ride. Get in the driver's seat. What do you want your reputation to be? What is the story you want others to be telling about you? Your story creates your platform for taking risks. Now go shape it!

Aspiration-to-Action

Craft your narrative using the template below as your guide. Remember to refer to the comprehensive template in this chapter for probing questions and tips to help you.

WHO you are

WHAT you do

WHY you do what you do

HOW you deliver value / make an impact

WHERE you want to go

Work with a partner to enhance your language. Try to find women who are more experienced to help you brainstorm, in addition to your *Begin Boldly* accountability advocate or friends, peers, and colleagues who have read this book. Look for ways to make things stronger through word choice and more memorable through anecdotes and stories. Remember the tips from this chapter: Highlight impact not just activities, use active powerful language rather than passive and powerless words, talk to results not just personal characteristics, and integrate some "I" language.

Practice articulating different aspects of your narrative. Work with a partner to play out different scenarios. They could ask you questions and role-play a networking event, an interview, or a casual meeting: "Stephanie, nice to meet you. Tell me about yourself." or "What are your immediate and long-term goals?" or "Tell me about how you drive value for the organization." These different questions and scenarios will encourage you to adapt your content to real-world settings and pick what works best for different audiences and conversations. Your partner can provide you with feedback to enhance your selection and delivery.

Risk-Reward-Refine-Repeat

Risk. Sharing your narrative can feel scary. Pick one person or situation where you'll come prepared to share aspects of your story. It could be one of the connectivity events you set up in a prior chapter. It could be at an upcoming interview. Pick one and remember to use your conversational tools from chapter 4 and ask the person about their story, as well as sharing yours.

> Complete the sentence: *The bold move I am going to commit to is sharing my narrative with _____ at _____.*

Reward. Did you experience any rewards (big or small) from sharing your narrative? Is someone in a decision-making role now aware of your interests? Did you have any connections facilitated for you?

Did someone indicate they would keep you in mind for future roles? Did you find a point of commonality or relation with your conversation partner? Capture what was beneficial from this experience, even if it's a lesson you learned from a conversation that could have gone better.

Refine. Reflect on how it went. How will you refine your approach to self-advocacy and sharing your narrative in future?

Repeat. Write down an upcoming situation, meeting, event, or conversation that you can plan for or seek out. Practice your narrative again, remembering to customize it for the audience and ask questions as well.

....

CHAPTER 9

Courageous Advocacy—
for Others

IF WE TRULY WANT TO EMPOWER WOMEN to live boldly and have brave careers, courageous advocacy can't stop with advocating for ourselves. It must include advocating for others. As the saying goes: Empowered women empower women. We can support the risk-taking of others by elevating them through using the power of our voices and the power of our choices.

During my first job after college, I was invited to speak at a women's conference. One of the other speakers shared this scenario that I now use in sessions that I run on allyship and advocacy.

Imagine that you're running to a critical client meeting where you're tasked with presenting the new proposal. This is a career-defining opportunity for you. You have so much on the line. You enter your building and dart to the elevator where you impatiently press the number of your floor. Just after pressing the button, you look up and see another woman running behind you, with a distressed face, desperately trying to get to the elevator before it closes. You now have a choice:

1— Press the "close doors" button to ensure waiting on someone else doesn't hold you up for this "mission critical" meeting.
2— Let fate run its course. Don't press any buttons. If the doors close, she's out of luck. If she makes it, good for her.
3— Proactively reach out and hold the door open with your arm to enable her access to the elevator so you can ascend together.

The question for you is: Who do you want to be? In the hustle and bustle of competing priorities, deadlines, career goals, and more, will you use your position of privilege in the elevator to help those around you and coming behind you? If you choose to wait, would you do so for any woman or only a select few that you know or can relate to?

While this may seem to be an easy choice, it's not always that easy to put into practice. And when we do, we often run into the trap of affinity bias. The key is to interrupt affinity bias through advocacy and create a powerful platform for other women to take risks.

/ **Challenge** / *Affinity bias (gravitating toward others like us) can negatively affect women in the workplace, particularly women who are underrepresented in their organization and teams. Affinity bias can affect all women; however, because of the existing demographic makeup of most workplaces, it often disproportionately affects women of color.*

Here are a number of ways affinity bias can hurt your career and the careers of other women around you.[68]

How we give feedback. Receiving specific and actionable feedback is essential to progressing in your career and improving. However, feedback providers, managers, reviewers, and leaders are more likely to give actionable feedback to those who are similar to them. If one of your peers isn't someone the feedback provider naturally gravitates toward, she may get vague feedback, which hinders her ability to grow, learn, and level up in her role. To make matters more complex, when providing feedback to a person of a different race, research has shown that the fear of being perceived as racist can creep in—which could keep a leader from sharing critical feedback or result in ambiguous feedback. In the end, women are less likely to get actionable feedback than their male peers, and the odds are even less favorable for women of color.

How we attribute successes and failures. Have you ever heard someone praised for their individual efforts and successes and another person's equally commendable success attributed to a team effort? This happens all the time. We're more likely to attribute the successes of someone like us to individual effort and the success of someone whom we perceive as different to a team effort.

Whom we hire. "This person will just be a great culture fit for the company." Have you ever heard a similar statement? This overused phrase of "fit" often appears to give others the permission to favor homogeneity over taking a risk on someone different. It disadvantages those who aren't "like us."

How we allocate work. We're more likely to give high-value or high-visibility assignments to people like us. Those we don't have an affinity with will not get the same opportunities.

Whom we hear in the room. Those who are perceived as different are less likely to have their ideas heard or get traction in group conversations. They are also more likely to be interrupted and talked over.

How we converse and connect. When we perceive differences, even our conversation changes. We will use more words and more positivity with someone with whom we have or perceive a similarity. Unfortunately, those whom we don't perceive as similar are more likely to get shorter conversations that come off as more negative. Similarity breeds familiarity, and this can have major implications for whether someone feels welcome in an organization.

Whom we sponsor or mentor. We know sponsorship is critical to career progression, as it offers visibility, relevant feedback, guidance; plugs people into opportunities; and provides the individual being sponsored with increased visibility and vocal advocacy. In a study published by the Center for Talent Innovation (CTI), now known as

Coqual, nearly three-quarters of executives sponsor individuals that mirror their own race and gender. The study, which surveyed more than 3,200 college-educated employees nationally who work in white-collar jobs, found that 71 percent of those who identified as sponsors said their protégé was the same race and gender as their own. It built on past research that had found 58 percent of women and 54 percent of men admitted to choosing a protégé because they "make me feel comfortable." CTI concluded: "People transfer power to others who make them feel comfortable."[69]

All of these factors above, when taken together, can make or break someone's career prospects.

Let's talk about how to make the road easier for those who may be on the same path but facing unique hurdles and obstacles due to perceived differences.

/ **Solution** / *Advocate for others through using the power of your choices and the power of your voice.*

The following tactics can be used regardless of your race or background or demographic makeup or level in an organization. The key is to use our voices and choices to elevate others. In addition, if you're personally facing these challenges, you can use this chapter to better understand how you can ask others for help and support. But don't abdicate your power to advocate for others. Even if we are personally grappling with some or all of these dynamics, we can't forget that we are all, regardless of background, role, hierarchy, level, race, ethnicity, disability, age, gender identity, sexual orientation, or religion, in a position to support other women. However, the actions we choose may depend on our own context and dynamics. The onus and responsibility to be the greatest advocates lie with the women who are in the majority in an organizational context, in a position of privilege, or both. For example, from a race perspective, in most settings, this is white women. In all settings, the greatest responsibility lies with those of us who are privileged to hold a position with power, influence, and access to the ears of decision-makers.

Remember: Performative advocacy is not advocacy. Saying you care about addressing inequities within your organization is not enough. A risk worth taking: advocating for others! The knock-on effect: They will be better positioned to take risks.

By reflecting on how to advocate for others, you are setting the stage for how you want others to advocate for you as well. Let's build a culture of advocacy. Let's elevate others and create an insurmountable tide of change where women rise and thrive within organizations through risk.

Put It into Practice

Give and request actionable feedback. When you provide feedback to others, ensure that it's actionable. When you see others receiving vague feedback, support them in their efforts to ask for more clarification and specific examples. You have the power to positively influence someone's career outcomes through this one simple act of advocacy. Make a conscious choice to give actionable feedback to all.

Highlight the successes of others. We know the successes of those who are underrepresented in the workplace may not be highlighted to the same extent as others, or they will be attributed to a team effort. Using your voice, you have the opportunity to point out and celebrate the wins of others. Increase the visibility of their progress and impact.

Encourage decision-makers to focus hiring discussions on criteria. In your early career years, you may not be involved in hiring decisions, but you may be (many early career individuals are involved in internship hiring efforts and campus recruitment). In most capacities, you'll have the opportunity to ask to understand hiring decisions and encourage that clear criteria be set (so that people aren't just hired due to a "hunch," "gut feeling," or because of perceived "culture fit"). If you're involved in the discussions, one powerful and simple way to ensure that decisions are defensible and focused on criteria (rather than emotion or affinity) is to ask questions. If someone makes a vague statement ("She's not a good fit for the company"), ask them why and why again, as it will push the conversation toward a concrete answer. This technique can help decision-makers to interrupt their own biases. Ask for evidence to back up assertions! Later on down the road, you can also use this approach in performance discussions. Using criteria is a choice that levels the playing field for those who are underrepresented.

Be mindful of how work is allocated. Depending on your level of influence over hiring decisions, you will likely be in discussions on who gets what role in a team, who is going to take on what responsibility, who is going to present or lead or take ownership of different aspects of a project. In these discussions, you have the ability to ask that decisions on high-value projects, roles, and responsibilities be focused on criteria (e.g., what is required for the role). You can be mindful of allocation of work and encourage others to be as well. You can ensure that the same go-to people are not consistently getting high-value and high-visibility opportunities while others are being overlooked. You can push for transparency around decision-making on who gets what role and why, and hold leaders to account.

Amplify the voices of others. Have you ever heard someone make a statement in a meeting and not be heard, and then ten minutes later someone else makes a similar statement or suggestion and the response is "Great idea!"? Have you heard someone offer insight, but no one responds or seems to have heard it? Have you ever heard someone be talked over or interrupted before they could fully express their viewpoint? This happens more in situations where there's perceived difference. The simple solution: Amplify the voices of others. For the first scenario, you could say: "I believe that is what Kristen was saying earlier. Kristen, could we go back to you? I'd love to hear more of what you were thinking." For the second, you could say something like: "Building on Kristen's idea, I wanted to explore whether we could talk about the potential to implement this in our current context." You simply use a bridge or beginning of a sentence that builds on the idea of the person whose voice may not have been heard in the room. For the last scenario, it can be as simple as "I think Kristen got cut off there and I'd like to hear the rest of her comment." Or, "I think Kristen was trying to share something. Kristen, can you repeat what you were saying?" This is tried and tested in real-world settings. During the Obama administration, women on Obama's staff made sure that their voices were heard through using the tactic of amplification.[71] They found that women were more likely to be interrupted or spoken over or not have their ideas heard. To combat this, they used amplification in meetings. When we were conducting our research, Lauren Noël and I interviewed Megan Costello, who was executive director of women's advancement for the City of Boston. She talked about using this practice: "We have to amplify other women's voices. If I am in a meeting and I see a female colleague struggling to make a point, sometimes I stop the meeting and say, 'I think Jane wants to say something. Jane, what were you just saying?'"[71]

Introduce colleagues, leading off with their credentials. We've already discussed the double bind women face: That women who are perceived to be tooting their own horn may be viewed as competent but not likable. The work-around? You toot the horn for other women! One simple action is to introduce women by leading off with their credentials (rather than asking them to introduce themselves). This could be applied at networking events, speaking events, meetings, new team introductions, and more. Will Rogers, the American stage and film actor, once said, "Get someone else to blow your horn and the sound will carry twice as far." This is even more true for women!

Check your "Outlook equity." We're more likely to spend time with people like us, who make us comfortable, who share an element of sameness. This can result in many employees feeling left out of important connections and networks, as outsiders who don't belong in certain settings and contexts. Knowing that it's natural to gravitate toward others who feel familiar, we need to make a conscious effort to bridge divides of difference and spend more time with people who may not be like us. This is one of the essential ways we can prevent "in-groups" and "out-groups" in organizations, enhance feelings of belonging, and ensure that important networks and connections are open to all employees. In a session I was recently running for a Fortune 500 company, the leaders encouraged their employees to "check their Outlook equity." I inquired what they meant by this, and they explained that they use the Microsoft Outlook platform and that asking employees to check their Outlook equity is asking them to see whom they are spending time with. Do they have an open-door policy only for some people? Are they responding to proactive employees rather than strategically setting up meetings and touch points with all team members? Are you investing time with some people more than others? Look at your "Outlook equity" or "calendar equity" and see how you can adjust how you spend your time. You can give yourself a challenge of inviting someone new to meetings or events where appropriate or setting up standing time slots where you connect with someone outside your normal circle. Tip: Once in the discussions or meetings, use your curious mindset to push the conversation forward, find points of relation and connectivity, and address inequities in conversation length and perceived positivity. It doesn't have to stop with you, either! You can encourage leaders to set up standing meetings or checkpoints with all team members, rather than simply responding to requests (that most often will come from the employees who feel most comfortable, while those who need the connection might not proactively reach out) or holding "office hours" (set times when people can drop in to see you) to create a true open-door policy.

Facilitate connections for others. Can you forge connections for others and help them cultivate a broad support network both inside and outside their organizations? My research with Lauren highlighted that when making decisions around whether to join or leave organizations, early career women placed a high priority on "connection." They wanted to "interact, collaborate, and build relationships with a dynamic network of peers, leaders, mentors, coaches, and sponsors."[72] We noted that a barrier to this for some women was affinity bias. How can you serve as a central point of connection for others? Bonus: Your social capital, trust, value, and career options will be enhanced if you act as a social connector. Endeavor to connect people and groups who don't know each other. How can you be a hub for others?

Help others enhance their narratives. Using the tools in the previous section, help others enhance their narratives. Through using more powerful action words, speaking to results and impact, with a mix of "I" and "we" language, and highlighting specific examples and anecdotes, you can help your peers create more compelling narratives. These narratives will help interrupt subjective judgments of "fit" and bolster credibility.

Open the Door and Level Up Others

These are simple and effective actions that you can take to be a powerful advocate for others. Advocating for others is a risk worth taking. Think about the woman in the elevator. Who do you want to be? I hope you hold the doors open!

Aspiration-to-Action

Reflect on a situation where affinity bias may have affected someone's experience at work (although you may not have realized it at the time). What was the situation? It could be a time someone wasn't heard in a room or was interrupted on calls. It could be someone not being considered for high-visibility roles. If helpful, you can do this exercise with a partner or your *Begin Boldly* accountability advocate to try to think reflectively about a time where affinity bias could have occurred. You can also think about a time when you may have been on the receiving end of the bias.

Reflect on what tactics from this chapter could have been used to interrupt the affinity bias: giving and requesting actionable feedback, highlighting the success of others, encouraging decision-makers to focus on criteria, being mindful of how work is allocated, amplifying the voices of others, introducing colleagues by leading off with their credentials, checking your "Outlook equity," facilitating connections for others. Capture your ideas.

Risk-Reward-Refine-Repeat

Risk. Now that we have looked back reflectively, think about an act of courageous advocacy you can take to address bias in your own teams and organization or institution. Choose one that feels risky for you, where you're putting yourself on the line for others and leveraging the power of your voice and choice to elevate others. Now take the risk!

Most of us have the power to advocate for others; however, if you feel in a disadvantaged position in your workplace, you could brainstorm one courageous act of advocacy that you'd like someone else to do that would have a big impact for you at work. You will have to make the ask and can reference chapter 5, on how to master "the art of the ask."

If both scenarios resonate (you can advocate but you also hope to be advocated for), come up with an answer for each.

Complete the sentences:
The bold moves I am going to commit to in order to advocate for others are...

The bold moves I am going to ask someone else to make to advocate for me are...

Reward. Some rewards may be experienced at a later date. If you're successful in building a culture of advocacy, you may not see returns for years to come: when more women stay with an organization and ascend into leadership roles or they transfer out for a leadership role in another organization. However, in the near term, you can assess rewards. Are more women being heard in the room? Are underrepresented women getting more high-profile opportunities? Are women getting the actionable feedback they need to be successful in their careers? Have you positively affected the career aspirations and prospects for one woman? These are all rewards!

If you have made the ask for advocacy, capture the impact of the advocacy action of others. Perhaps you feel that you're getting more actionable feedback, having your views heard more, or being considered for high-value assignments.

Refine. Use the try-it-and-tweak-it approach. Test these approaches and see what the results are. Use the data to improve how you advocate for others and how you ask others to advocate for you in the future. What did you learn? How will you refine your advocacy approach?

Repeat. What advocacy actions are you going to take next? Are there any advocacy asks you're going to make next? What are you going to repeat?

PART IV

THE AGILE MINDSET

· · · · · · · · ·

Many of life's greatest opportunities and rewarding moments are plot twists in your journey. To truly be open to the risks inherent in these plot twists, you must embrace the unexpected. Lives and careers are dynamic, with so many influencing and ever-changing variables. If the COVID-19 era has taught us anything, it's that we can't control everything that shapes our career context, so we need to focus on what we can control: our agility. The more flexible you can be during times of change, the better.

Agility, flexibility, and adaptability in the face of uncertainty, change, and new opportunities will be critical to your ability to embrace adventure and risk and to build a career that you love. One female executive I interviewed in London referred to her agility as her inner game, what she can control. "How good I am at my inner game determines my outer game, which is the impact I have, the difference I make."[73] Building a life and career you love is an ongoing journey, a process of continuous improvement. Master your agile mindset to experiment and build a dynamic identity that evolves as you do. As Jack Zenger, the author of the *Harvard Business Review* article "How Age and Gender Affect Self-Improvement," says: "Career success is driven by a person's ability to constantly learn and adapt to a changing world. Doing so takes the right mindset."[74] This is what I term an agile mindset.

....

CHAPTER 10

Agile Experiments

ONE KEY TO RISKING SUCCESSFULLY is realizing that your life and career are in a constant state of experimentation. Trying new things and taking risks can be scary, especially early in your career when you're making first impressions and working hard to establish a good reputation. To put your ideas into practice and bridge the gap between aspiration and action, you can use "agile experimentation": small, clearly defined experiments with short turnaround times and measurable indicators of success. You can craft and customize these experiments strategically while taking into account your organization's culture and engaging the appropriate colleagues, mentors, or leaders (your Support). This allows you to try out new things on a smaller scale before making greater leaps and larger changes. The idea of experimentation is not new: I leverage the work and ideas of organizational psychologists, such as Stew Friedman, and the advice of many other thought leaders who have discussed taking a start-up, entrepreneurial, and experimental approach to your life. But what's differentiated here is the power of this enhanced and tweaked approach specifically for women, taking into account the gender lens and how this approach targets what is holding women back. Harness your curious and courageous mindsets and embrace a constant state of experimentation to master the art of risk-taking. Effective experimentation takes curiosity, courage, and agility. Let's get started.

/ **Challenge** / *Making a big change can be daunting, whether it's in relation to your career or to a proposed changes within your organization.*

This feeling of intimidation can often lead to inaction, which can have long-term implications for your career.

Moving to another country, putting yourself up for a promotion, applying for a new job, making a career move, going back to school, transitioning to part-time work, asking for a virtual work arrangement, requesting an internal transfer or role change, starting your own business: all of these big moves can be overwhelming for most individuals.

Over years of working with young women, and having been through the journey myself, I've seen a trend where there's the tendency to overanalyze, overthink, and often get caught in a stagnant state of *analysis paralysis*. In other words, you become unable to take action, feel paralyzed and stagnant, due to overanalyzing seemingly large risks.

I remember finishing my second master's degree at the University of Oxford on the Rhodes Scholarship and telling my partner at the time, who's now my husband, that I wasn't sure what I wanted to do professionally. Because of the recession, I didn't have a clear sense of the job I wanted or the direction I wanted to take. I knew what I was passionate about but not what work would be right for me. I was reading, analyzing, talking to people, and felt overwhelmed by information. I lacked internal clarity. But that clarity wasn't going to come from inner reflection in the absence of outward action. My partner looked at me and said: "You're not going to know until you try." This was such a simple statement but so powerful. He stressed that I wasn't going to have an epiphany around exactly what I wanted to do. Instead, knowing and self-knowledge come through trying. Although I didn't know it at the time, his guidance was aligned with the work of Herminia Ibarra, a professor of organizational behavior at London Business School. She encourages us to experiment with a "repertoire of possibilities" within our professional sphere until experience shows which one fits our situation best.[75] Rather than falling victim to analysis paralysis and therefore delayed action, we are told by Herminia Ibarra, that thinking and introspection should follow action and experimentation. Not vice versa. Instead of analyzing then acting, we should act then analyze. Over time, working with clients, I realized that analysis without action has its limitations and that we should err on the side of earlier action through agile experimentation. My husband's advice and Herminia Ibarra's work have encouraged me to take bolder action sooner, rather than getting stuck in the overthinking sinkhole and struggling to climb out. I hope you're ready to do the same!

Before we begin, it's important to clarify that a certain amount of thinking and preparation can be helpful. But thinking has its limits. Learning truly happens through action. Unfortunately, many women are afraid to take action and justify delay with "I need to think or know or analyze more before making the leap or decision."

We don't need an all-or-nothing approach: I'm going to leave my career or I'm going to stay; I'm going to ask the company to change its flexible work policy or I'm going to keep on working the way I am; I'm going to take on a new role within my organization or I'm not; I'm going to leave my job to start an entrepreneurial venture or I'm going to stay here for the foreseeable future. Don't fall victim to a life of extremes—of all-or-nothing options—that create false dichotomies and promote inaction (we will talk ourselves out of doing something before we even try). There is a better approach: agile experimentation.

Agile experimentation is, once again, based on what I term "the early career progress principle": start small, then scale. The key is to think about how you can experiment with small-scale changes to give you the insights you need to decide whether to make bigger and bolder leaps. The trick to moving past overanalysis and paralysis: adopting the spirit of experimentation in your life. The solution is trying things on a small scale before you move forward.

Think back to Nim De Swardt. The former chief next generation officer of Bacardi Global recommends adopting an experimental approach to your career and life. "You must have the courage to take risks and pilot new methods, while being innately curious with a penchant for start-up-style experimentation in your own organization, your own career, and your own life." It was this experimentation approach that led Nim to explore so many different interests, from innovation to generations to environmental conservation to story-telling and more, which helped her build her dynamic, ever-evolving, and exciting career.

/ **Solution** / *Start with small agile experiments and then scale.*

One of my clients was dealing with daily frustrations. "Our meetings are inefficient. We're all over the place. We're lacking time; it's so unproductive and it's creating politics and causing conflict amongst our teams." She wasn't comfortable or in a position to propose herself as the one to lead these meetings; however, I pushed her on what approaches she could try. "What if you experimented with asking for agendas from all contributors in a meeting beforehand and ensuring action items are captured on the back end of the meeting? Let's try it for a few weeks. We can touch base and see if the meetings have been more effective and more efficient. If they haven't been, experimenting with this approach will help us isolate why and see if you can tweak this moving forward. If they have improved, it might be something you can propose more broadly to the company for other meetings, with the proof point that you've tried this in your meetings with good results."

This is a small but significant example of how to experiment within your organization. Many women I've worked with and interviewed have noted the importance of starting small. For instance, one junior associate, who was a year out of law school and social-media savvy, took on managing a social media platform of the organization, a small, distinct task with measurable outputs. Perhaps this woman wasn't ready to put herself up for a lead social media role, but by trying a distinct project, she showcased her ability to implement new approaches and get results. The executive who shared this story noted the measurable impact on increasing followers that this woman had. Is there a small committee, project, or process that you could experiment with at your company?

Let's take a look at some bigger career risks that can be broken down to a short-term, agile experimentation. Imagine you're considering transitioning from the corporate world into social work. Instead of having to make a huge leap or getting stuck in research mode, could you volunteer on weekends or after work at a center or with a social work team and then, after a defined period of time, assess what learnings you have about yourself and this potential career move? Another example: What if you're considering going back to school to become a dietician? That can be a big leap and longer-term commitment. What if you started off with an experiment: a short-term certificate program or shadowing someone? Agile experimentation makes it possible to try it before you deny it!

It's useful to refer to chapter 5 on curiosity and influence, as agile experimentation is also a powerful tool in building buy-in when making an ask. Imagine that you'd like a more flexible working schedule. Instead of saying "I want to revamp our entire working schedule," you can use your curious mindset from part 2 to share the problem that you've identified or the current issue and a potential solution you think would be worth trying. Instead, you could say, "What if I experimented with this new schedule for a month and continue to measure the metrics that matter to our team (hours worked, employee satisfaction, meeting client deadlines)? At the end of the month, we can check in on the results that matter most and then we'll see how we're doing. If it doesn't work, then I'm happy to go back to the original schedule or to tweak our approach based on the insights we've gained." Experimentation and the insights allow us to continue to evolve and improve how we live, work, and contribute to any context of which we are a part.

I've seen this work particularly well for women who are negotiating for more control over where and when they work. They might say: "I'd like to work virtually for these days and I'd like to try it for a month, see whether we're able to still deliver on what matters to our clients and the team, and then we can either continue or adjust from there. If there are any issues, then we can course correct." This experimental approach has so many wins. It helps you address your own fears, which will be especially rife in an all-or-nothing approach. When you're able to do things on a smaller scale, you overcome some of that fear of that big leap or big step because you know you can try it and tweak it! It helps you get out of your own head and choose exper-imental action and learning over analysis paralysis. Additionally, it helps you build buy-in. Although research is incredibly valuable, a lot of things in life are trial and error. Experimentation is a tool in your kit that you can use strategically to learn through doing.

Senior-level leaders also appreciate the value of an experimen-tal approach when it comes to seeking solutions to organizational challenges or maximizing opportunities. Leena Nair led the charge to reinvent Unilever's recruiting of college graduates. She shared that the recruitment process is now entirely digitized. To apply to work for the company, applicants play twelve games for two minutes each, upload a selfie video, and go through a discovery center, all accessed digitally. When I interviewed her in 2017, the initiative had already been a huge success. More than 250,000 people had applied, 3,500 applicants had been interviewed, and 800 people had been selected to work at Unilever under the new approach. She acknowledged: "Disrupting the recruitment process was a risk. But because I am ready to embrace failure, more people applied to work at Unilever. Learn to pilot, experiment, and do early tests. What's the worst that can happen? It can flop and we can go back to doing three interviews per applicant. If you don't take risks, you don't move forward."[76] Even in her senior leadership role, she leveraged the power of experimen-tation to try new approaches while building buy-in. Experimenting when you're in your early career years will help you build these skills so that when you're in senior leadership, and have more power and a greater stage on which to work, you've optimally developed your skill of experimentation.

Others can be resistant to change and to risk. Most people like to cling to how things are done now and what they're comfortable with. If you propose broad-scale change, you can face some resistance. But proposing short-term experiments or trials with agreed-on goals and measures of success will help address the barriers. Just frame it as Nair did: "Let's see how it works!" Very few people will say no to a small-scale trial.

Put It into Practice

Use a tried-and-tested approach to guide your experimentation.
Figure 1 presents a tried-and-tested framework to start planning
your agile experiments. It leverages key components of the risk-taking models of Risk-Reward-Refine-Repeat and Bold MOVES, but it's
calibrated to be more project-focused so that you can present this in
workplace environments as a method you're using to problem-solve
and experiment. If you notice that the basic fundamentals are the
same, you're right! The inquiry stage requires a curious mindset,
the ideation stage pushes you to explore bold possibilities, experimentation requires courage, and evolving based on the outcomes of
the experiment is based on the enduring principles in this book of
continuous improvement and an ongoing journey of risking. These
experiments in your workplace context are one type of risk you can
take in the first step of your Risk-Reward-Refine-Repeat model.

Figure 1: The Cycle of Agile Experimentation

Isolate Intent
What is your 'why'?
Why is this important to
you/your organization?

**Agile
Experimentation**
©Christie Hunter Arscott

Evolve

Inquire

Experiment

Ideate

**Measure
Outcomes/Impact**
Use data as insights to
fuel improvement!

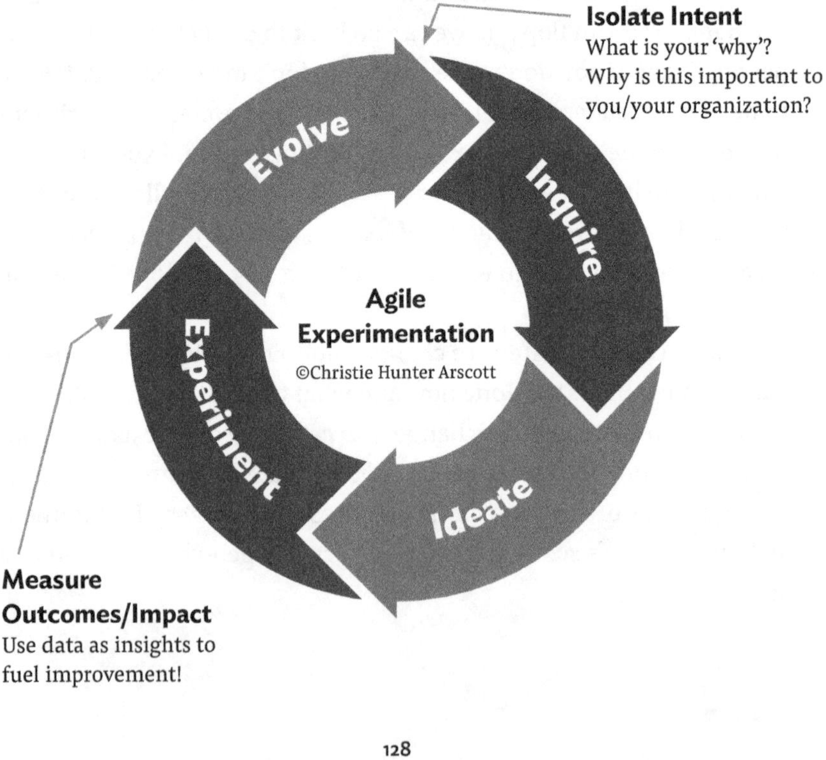

The first step, **inquire**, is really where you harness your curious mindset (from part 2). Here are some critical questions you can ask during the initial process of inquiry.

- What is the problem or opportunity?
- Why is this important? Why do I want to solve this problem or make the most of this opportunity? *Hint:* Identifying intent is important! See the specific call out on the agile experimentation model.
- What do we know already?
- What are our unknowns?
- Has this arisen before?
- Has it been addressed before, either successfully or unsuccessfully? And, if yes, what can we learn from the past approach?
- Are there comparable situations or contexts we can learn from? Maybe there are other situations or other companies that have solved similar problems that you can refer to and say: What is it that we might be able to learn here? What is it that may or may not apply to our distinct situation? Remember: You have the power to leverage the learnings of others through harnessing your curious mindset while implementing agile experiments.

For instance, I was working with one organization that was struggling to figure out how to start its Diversity and Inclusion initiative. Instead of saying "This is what I think you should do," I asked, "What initiatives have been successful in your company and why? What was their structure?" And the response was "Ahhh, you're right. You know, we have a corporate social responsibility initiative that was set up with a forum of different leaders, in different offices globally, and if we said we were leveraging a similar model that already works for us, that would build stakeholder buy-in and get us the kind of traction we need to implement this diversity initiative."

Inquiry is so important because we can sometimes end up irrationally rushing to a solution rather than using the process of inquiry to push ourselves and our teams further.

The next step, **ideate**, encourages you to think boldly and bravely about what solutions you could explore. Write them down, using post-its or an online tool to map ideas. Harness the ideas of those around you. Think about you and your teams as an innovation hub with the potential to generate new and exciting approaches and ideas. Push them to think by asking questions: What potential solutions can we generate to solve this issue? What can we explore?

Again, don't focus on any concerns about "how" you will implement solutions. Many great ideas get squashed because of feasibility concerns when it would be better to brainstorm big and then filter based on practicality among other factors. Right now is the time to remember why this is important and what you may want to try. What are the possibilities? What are the solutions?

The next step, **experiment**, also starts with critical questions: What solutions are we going to try? For how long? In what setting? How will we measure success? I often see women fall into the trap of an all-or-nothing approach, for instance, "I am either pursuing this course or not." What typically happens then is that the idea of heading down one path without an out becomes so overwhelming that they shy away from pursuing a solution. The trick to address this is to adopt a spirit of experimentation, knowing that you can try and test approaches and changes, and then course correct as needed. This is the very essence of being agile. You can give something a try in a less risky environment or on a smaller scale before thinking about a more permanent change. For instance, let's say you have an idea on how your team can work smarter or more efficiently. Instead of asking for a change for the indefinite future, you could propose: What if we tried working and communicating like this for the next month? We could track our progress and efficiency and the quality of work, as well as if it alleviates stress for our team. After a month, we can touch base with everyone to see what's working and whether we should continue like this, tweak our approach, or revert to the old ways of doing things.

The great news: whatever you learn through experimentation helps you **evolve**. Evolving is about understanding that we're not trying to get things 100 percent right every single time and that experimentation gives us data to fuel our ongoing improvement and evolution. Reflect on what you've learned from experimentation. Will you abandon this idea as a solution? If so, what have you learned from this attempt? Will you give it more time? Will you push forward with it? Will you evolve an existing solution by tweaking your approaches with the data that you have gathered? A commitment to evolving helps us battle an inclination for perfection because we recognize that lifelong learning requires constant curiosity, experimentation, tweaking, and evolving.

You can bring this model to your work, to your teams, and to your organization as a way to push forward conversations and help yourself and others move from not seeing problems until they hit you in the face to proactively being future-focused and identifying problems and ideating solutions before you even realize that you have an issue. It is a powerful formula that uses your agile mindset to inquire, ideate, experiment, and evolve.

Word of caution: New hires should be cautious not to come across as arrogant. ("I know this organization better than you and have identified issues you don't even know you have!") Remember to make this a collaborative effort and approach and communicate strategically. You can use some of the communication approaches outlined in chapter 5, on using curiosity as a tool of influence, such as strategic questioning, and engage key stakeholders upfront by asking for their opinions and insights.

Start small. Building your experimentation skills takes time, as does moving past fear and uncertainty. A great way to start is to go small. Don't underestimate the impact of seemingly small-scale experiments. In one situation, an early career woman working at a medical office shared with her manager: "I see room for improvement at the front desk." She went on to elaborate that what she had noticed wasn't an issue yet but could become one. She noted that providers and staff were giving patients different recommendations and that there was a lack of alignment on best treatment protocols. While there hadn't been any patient complaints, she noted that there could be in the future. She suggested that she build out "scripts" based on areas of patient concern so that every provider could refer to a standard set of protocols. The team could experiment with this approach, track patient feedback, and then tweak as needed. This is a perfect example of a seemingly small experiment that could have a huge impact in the long run on patient experience, efficiency, consistency, sales, and more. She proactively identified a problem and suggested an experiment that she could execute on. Small experiments and big wins!

When you're thinking about problem-solving, don't just think about the brand of your company, its target markets, your mission, and the internal policies. Think about how you can problem-solve in day-to-day interactions and with your teams. Nora Abd Manaf, group chief human capital officer, Maybank Group, based in Malaysia, advises being a relentless and creative problem-solver and experimenter: "The world has enough people who point out problems."[77] Be the one who asks critical questions and provides a viewpoint on the solutions.

Define your experiment. If you're truly a creative and innovative person but your role doesn't allow for you to use these skills, could you propose to spend five or maybe even ten hours a week on new ideas or strategic projects? You can try it for a month and ensure that you're still delivering on core responsibilities. If training for a specific sport is a priority, could you work with leaders to design a month-long experiment where you leave early to make practice and then get online later, working remotely from home? Are you interested in a temporary assignment to another team for exposure and learning or an increased work schedule with the goal of accelerated promotion? Are you interested in contributing to internal Diversity and Inclusion initiatives? Do you have an idea on how your company could reach new markets or consumers? Perhaps you see an opportunity to try out an experiment related to shortening manufacturing times, creating more lean and efficient processes, or increasing sales. Do you believe that there's a way to run a better meeting, to improve communication, to manage client demands more efficiently, to develop new ways of working? As long as you define it as an experiment or trial, have a set time frame, and are tracking success metrics that are important to you and others, such as your manager, partner, family, and business, then you have the opportunity to go for it!

Build buy-in. Applying the framework referenced in this chapter can be useful to build buy-in with others, and yourself, if you're struggling with the thought of making sweeping, longer-term changes. With others, the most important aspect is sharing your "intent" (why this is important) and reiterating that this is an "experiment." Worst-case scenario, it doesn't work, and it's only been a month of trying something new. Best-case scenario, you enhance how you live and work, and have insights to fuel the ongoing refinement of your model or experiment.

Measure what matters. Whether you're designing and executing experiments in your personal or your professional realm, engage the people who matter in the process of defining what matters to them while you define what matters to you. Align on what success looks like, and then after a set period of time, examine outcomes related to these indicators.

For success metrics, you can complete the sentence:
The experiment will be successful if...

These, of course, will be context dependent and could include (depending on the experiment) the following success indicators:

- Clients have faster turnaround times.
- Internal innovation is up (we're getting more ideas from our people).
- Followers have increased.
- Brand recognition improves.
- Employee engagement is higher.
- Teams are increasingly diverse.
- Team productivity is higher.
- Key stakeholders have provided positive feedback.

- Performance improves.
- There is better differentiation from competitors.

Define what matters most and measure it to evaluate your experiment and then evolve the project with these insights to fuel improvement.

Create Your Proof of Concept

In closing this chapter, I want to share a story about when I was completing a business certification at Stanford Graduate School of Business. A speaker came in and said: "We should be applying business skills to social issues." I began thinking about the transferability of business skills to other realms of life and work. What I realized is that new start-ups, entrepreneurs, and businesses frequently pilot something prior to a broader rollout to test the market and get meaningful data about what model will work. Their experimentation creates an initial proof of concept, verifying that an idea or approach has practical potential before they scale. We need to apply this experimental approach of try-it-and-tweak-it to our own careers and lives.

Aspiration-to-Action

Identify areas where you might be able to try small-scale experiments to address a defined or anticipated need or problem. At this beginning stage of your career, or at the start of any experimentation, I suggest trying something within your control that doesn't need sign-off from a manager and then progressing to something where you need approval. For instance, you could experiment with trying new meeting structures or with setting up regular touch points with team members to ensure that everyone is aligned on priorities. You could experiment with new ideas on how to increase traffic to your platforms or better meet the needs of your clients. You got this!

Risk-Reward-Refine-Repeat

Risk. Identify a problem you'd like to solve or an opportunity you'd like to maximize in your career context or organization. Start by framing the opportunity, conducting inquiry (including pinpointing your intent), and ideating on solutions and options you could try or pilot. Share your idea with a confidant to keep you accountable and also get the insights of others, such as a mentor, colleague, manager, or peer. Then take the plunge to experiment and use your insights to evolve. This can feel risky at first and you may feel out of your depth, but remember: It's just an experiment!

Complete the sentence: *The bold move I am going to commit to in my career is developing an experiment related to...*

Reward. Did you experience any rewards from this exercise? How did you evolve?

Refine. Once you have executed your experiment, think about how you would refine your approach moving forward. What worked? What didn't? Will you abandon the approach, continue using it, or tweak it to improve it? What did you learn, and how will you apply these learnings to a future experiment or iteration of the same experiment? Remember that experimentation is a process of continuous improvement.

Repeat. Are you ready to try experiments in other areas? Are you ready to refine this experiment? Decide how you will continue to practice the experimental approach to risk-taking!

....

CHAPTER 11

Agile Identity

YOU HAVE THE OPPORTUNITY to shape your identity, which in turn influences your trajectory. My work has shown that careers are contingent on identity and can expand or contract depending on how you define yourself. Limited views of self can heighten risk aversion and in turn stunt career growth. Expansive, flexible, and evolving views of self can positively influence your appetite for risk, as well as create expansive and exciting careers. In essence: the view you have of yourself has the power to define your career and life. Carol Dweck, the renowned psychologist and Stanford professor, said: "For twenty years, my research has shown that the view you adopt for yourself profoundly affects the way you lead your life. It can determine whether you become the person you want to be and whether you accomplish the things you value." Ask yourself: Will my career be limited or limitless? The great news: It's up to you to influence this outcome.

/ **Challenge** / *Women can fall victim to defining themselves in limiting and fixed terms, which holds them back from realizing the bold careers of which they're capable.*

Self-doubt for women often manifests in the form of limited identities and beliefs. If you have ever heard your inner voice say statements involving extremes such as "I can't ...," "I'll never ...," and "I will always ...," you're likely falling victim to a rigid identity fueled by self-doubt. These are internal barriers to our own success, as they hinder risk-taking and also impede improvements and growth. My study revealed that in addition to fear of failure, self-doubt is the other primary factor that deters women from taking intelligent risks that will propel their careers forward. When I asked women, "If you have avoided risks, what factors and reasons contributed to this?," "self-doubt" (not having enough belief in myself, my capabilities, and skills) came in second only to "fear of failure," with over 70 percent of respondents reporting this as a critical deterrent. Further analysis revealed that this self-doubt stems from fixed, rigid, and limited beliefs about who one is (identity) and what one is capable of. As James Clear, the award-winning author of *Automatic Habits*, says: "The more you let a single belief define you, the less capable you are of adapting when life challenges you."[78]

Instead of focusing on improving, learning, and adapting, women with limited definitions of self are more prone to believe that their abilities are inborn or innate and unlikely to change. These identities are the opposite of agile; they are inflexible, rigid, and not malleable, or as Dweck says, "Fixed."

While Dweck's work speaks to women having fixed views on capabilities, skills, and identities, the work of Jack Zenger, the leadership development expert, builds on these concepts and highlights another concerning trend for women. His analysis of over seven thousand self-assessments of women and men highlights that women in their earlier career stages are more likely than men to avoid challenging situations, feedback, and criticism and to play it safe by seeking tasks in which they look good and succeed. Women are more likely than men to lack a focus on improving. While over 50 percent of men in the study focused on improving throughout their early career years, the majority of women didn't transition to focusing on improvements until their fifties.[79] The older you get, the more likely you are to focus on self-improvement, but it's often too little, too late.

/ **Solution** / *Let go of the limiting beliefs that are holding you back.*

Behavioral changes are inextricably linked to belief changes. Embracing risk-taking behaviors starts with changing beliefs and narratives that limit rather than liberate. Realize that our identities aren't fixed but fluid. You can redefine yourself at any time, knowing that you're flexible enough to be transformed into a new and better version of yourself if you commit to continuous learning and improvement. A growth orientation is critical to making the most of your early career years, and a focus on growth and improvements can't exist without an agile identity. You "have to be adaptable. I always tell my team that they have to love the color grey. Embrace the grey,"[80] says Kristen Robinson, formerly senior vice president of digital experience at Fidelity and now chief operating officer of Fidelity Charitable.

Put It into Practice

Move past self-doubt. Here's a quick way to address your doubts. Think about how you would finish the following sentences: "I'm not good at . . . ." "I can't do . . . ." "I'll always struggle with . . . ." "I could never . . . ." These are self-limiting beliefs (assumptions or perceptions that you have about yourself) that become self-limiting because in some way they're holding you back from achieving what you're truly capable of. Identifying them is key to moving forward. The bad news: If you accept a self-limiting belief, it will become a truth for you (a self-fulfilling prophecy). For example,

1— You believe a lie about yourself: "I'm just not good at networking."

2— You self-sabotage: Avoiding networking events (which would allow you to practice and improve your skills).

3— You reinforce the lie because of "proof": Going to a networking event, fumbling over your words, feeling nervous and embarrassed, telling yourself "I told you so." Then you reinforce the lie because of proof ("I knew I was bad at networking and now I've shown myself this is true").

It's a vicious cycle. These beliefs and doubts are the balls and chains holding us back from realizing our true potential and best careers.

The good news: you can interrupt these thoughts in a few simple steps.

Recognize. Recognize when you're thinking a limiting belief or grappling with self-doubt. A red flag should go up when you hear or think the words "I can't," "I will never," or "I always."

Remember your reason. Envision your life without these limiting beliefs: What would you be doing? Whom would you be surrounding yourself with? What would you be achieving? How would you be feeling? This helps you summarize why you want to overcome this belief, and you can return to this vivid imagery when you feel self-doubt rearing its ugly head.

Counteract confirmation bias. Confirmation bias means that we're more likely to look for examples that reinforce our limiting beliefs and negative biases about ourselves than to seek out or see examples that counter them. If you say, "I'll never be a good networker," think of times when you have made meaningful connections, chatted with others, and built relationships. These will help you realize that limiting beliefs aren't facts. Look for evidence that proves that your extreme thinking has cracks! If you're struggling with this, pair up with a partner, friend, close contact, or mentor. They can help you look at your past behaviors and patterns and may see things you don't.

Replace. Try replacing your old belief with a new one: "I will always be terrible at networking" with "I am not great at networking yet" or "I know being a great connector takes practice and I will practice more." Remember that we are all fluid, not fixed. Great athletes, communicators, leaders are not born; they are made.

Reposition. If you do fail, answer: "What would I say to a friend in this situation?" You will show more compassion and less judgment. The next time you take a risk and mess up, or make a mistake, or don't do as well as you would have liked, can you say something to yourself that's less condemning and more supportive?

Risk (and repeat). Risking is key to getting comfortable with being uncomfortable and moving past self-doubt and internal resistance. It's essential to building your agile and ever-changing and adapting identity. In her book, *Big Magic*, Elizabeth Gilbert shared that she always had to do what she dreaded most: "Scared of the ocean? Get in the ocean."[81] It was risking that allowed limitations to be challenged and identities to be expanded.

Flip the script from "Why me?" to "Why not me?" One powerful trick I've learned from the women I've researched is learning how to flip the script as a method of moving beyond fixed and limited identities to increase action and appetite for risk. This action interrupts unhelpful beliefs and reframes your internal dialogue as you consider whether to take a risk.

For example, in 1991, the chief operating officer of the Federal Reserve Bank of Boston was retiring. As a result, the Boston Fed was in search of a new COO. Cathy Minehan had worked at the Federal Reserve Bank of New York for twenty-four years. There had never been a woman COO at any Federal Reserve Bank at that time, but that didn't stop Minehan from putting herself forward for the position. "By that time, I had managed every operation at the Fed of New York. So, I called the president of the Boston Fed and said: 'I know you are looking for a chief operating officer. Why don't you interview me?'"[82] He replied that he had not considered Minehan for the position but agreed to meet her for dinner to discuss. She interviewed and got the job.

Minehan's promotion to COO was groundbreaking. This "Why not me?" mindset is typical of women who have built brilliant careers. It's an effective way to balance out the natural tendency to limit oneself.

Try flipping the script from Why me? to Why not me? to build an agile identity and increase your appetite for risk.

Break through the Bars

Imagine that your limiting beliefs and your fixed identity are the bars of a self-created jail cell. Do they keep you safe? Yes. However, they also keep the rest of the world out, all the opportunity, possibilities, and potential. Rather than defining yourself narrowly, you have the opportunity, the power, and the tools to break out and define yourself in expansive and fluid ways. Embracing an agile identity will position you to seek risks outside your own self-imposed limitations and realize that we are all evolving, growing, and changing throughout our career journeys. We are fluid, not fixed, with endless possibilities for our careers. We are all works in progress!

Aspiration-to-Action

Recognize. What is the one limiting belief that holds you back the most? What is the limiting belief you cling to, a narrative you tell about yourself, that limits your identity and growth?

Remember your reason. Envision your life without that limiting belief. What you would be doing, how you would be feeling, what you would be achieving. Close your eyes and picture it. Then write it down.

In addition to working toward this vision, capture additional reasons why you may want to overcome this limiting belief. What is your 'why?'

Tip: I heard Dr. Elizabeth Lombardo, a psychologist and the author of *Better Than Perfect*, speak at a conference years ago. Her advice: Make sure your 'whys' (reasons for wanting this goal) outweigh your 'buts' (the obstacles that are present).

Counteract confirmation bias. What are examples that may counter this limiting belief? Are there times when your limiting belief was not true? Capture them. These are pieces of evidence that show that your extreme thinking might not be 100 percent accurate.

Replace. What language would you use to replace your old belief with a new one? What's your new focus? As Gilbert notes: "Argue for your limitations and you get to keep them."[83] Instead, I encourage you to replace them.

Reposition. The next time you take a risk and mess up, or make a mistake, or don't do as well as you would have liked to, what will you say to yourself? Pretend you're talking to a friend.

························ **Risk–Refine–Reward–Repeat** ························

Risk. Get comfortable being uncomfortable. What are two or three risks, or smaller courageous acts, you can take over the next three months that are related to your limiting belief? If this belief is around connecting with others, what events can you go to? If it's about speaking in front of people, can you offer to present to your team?

Complete the sentence: *The bold moves I am going to commit to are...*

Reward. What rewards have been produced as a result of taking these risks? Even if the risk didn't go as well as expected, think about your reward as what you learned and how this will affect your growth moving forward. Does your limiting belief stand up to scrutiny? Have you realized that you're more capable of networking or speaking than you thought? Did you try something new and not do well? What did you learn? Were your limiting beliefs called into question? If yes, how?

Refine. How has taking these risks helped you refine your approach to tackling your limiting beliefs and building a more agile identity?

Repeat. We conjure up limiting beliefs throughout our entire lives. Taking risks to build a less-limited and more agile and expansive identity is an exercise that you can do again and again. Core limiting beliefs tend to crop up over the decades, and new ones arise of which we become conscious. Repeat. Repeat. Repeat.

Tip: It's best to do this exercise with your *Begin Boldly* accountability advocate, who can hold you accountable for taking the risks and help you interrupt your own limiting beliefs (by helping you see situations and contexts where your extreme views aren't accurate). You can both capture the risks that your partner is committing to and set up a checkpoint to reconnect on what risks you took, what rewards you experienced, how they refined your viewpoints on your limiting beliefs and approaches to risk, and how you will repeat.

CHAPTER 12

Agile Change

LIFE IS FLUID, with constant challenges and opportunities large and small that you're going to face both inside and outside the workplace. Whether it's an unexpected restructuring of your organization, a critical team member leaving your company, a merger or acquisition, a loss of funding, a new strategic direction, a shift in leadership priorities, a promotion, a family emergency, or a job loss, change is unavoidable. It's in global health crises and the economic and social implications they create for communities, organizations, families, and individuals. It's in social justice movements that catalyze changes to how we live, work, and interact. The list is endless. Change is both inevitable and scary. Being an intelligent risk-taker involves embracing change and having faith in your capability to figure things out, regardless of the outcome. By adopting an agile approach to change, you'll practice moving forward with incomplete information in the face of uncertainty and swapping the comfort of control for the freedom to discover and explore the realm of possibilities while embracing change.

/ **Challenge** / *Women, particularly in the earlier stages of their careers, often underestimate their ability to manage change.*

My coaching client was dealing with a period of unprecedented change in her organization. The company was going through a merger, her direct boss was leaving, the pressures on her team were shifting, the reporting structures were in flux, and the dynamics between the teams of the two organizations involved in the merger were tense. Like many women I work with, she was overwhelmed, scared, and grasping for a sense of control. "I'm just not good with change," she said. This is such a common way that women self-describe their struggle with change.

Our first reaction to change that seems outside our control can be anxiety, fear, and dread. This response can cause a fight-or-flight response where we either want to fight the change or leave the situation altogether. We focus on what we can lose or what might go wrong while underestimating our ability to handle changes. My work has reinforced that unexpected change can elicit feelings of helplessness and emotional overwhelm for women, as they continually underestimate their ability to rise to the challenges that change produces. My studies showed that some women shy away from risk-taking because of the changes it could produce and the fact that they desire to focus on what they can control rather than embrace uncertainty. Only 19 percent of women reported that they're comfortable with change and uncertainty when taking a risk. Building your comfort with change is an essential part of building your risk-taking skill.

/ **Solution** / *Claim your reaction to change as a "choice."*

Externally imposed change can sometimes interfere with feelings of autonomy and make you feel that you've lost control. However, autonomy, ownership, and empowerment come from choice in the face of change. Despite discomfort with change, those who have paved bold and brilliant career paths attribute it partly to their ability to not just manage change but also to embrace it and control their reactions to it. One female executive shared that when she was a child, her family moved frequently and she attended thirteen schools before graduating high school. "It pushed me to embrace change, which has been helpful professionally. We are always adapting to change from our clients and re-thinking the way our practice works. Being adaptable to change is such a critical part of keeping pace with a fast-paced industry."[84] Other pioneering women shared that it's important to be open to change and take risks. The two go hand in hand.

Many of the female executives with whom I've interacted have encouraged others to throw away the script. Career paths take twists and turns. Often, these detours turn out to be some of the most rewarding and valuable experiences of professional and personal lives. "Life is not a movie script that you write and then have everybody else act in it," explains Margie Yang, chairwoman of Esquel Group, the world's largest woven-shirt maker. "Don't be a control freak.... [unexpected changes] could turn out to be wonderful surprises that you never expected."[85]

Put It into Practice

Take the victim out and put the power of choice in. While change can elicit feelings of helplessness, the stories above teach us that we have control over how we respond. We can focus on our own agile mindset and understand that we have a distinct choice in how we react to change. Change can either happen to us, where we are the passive pawn, or change can happen within us, where we take control over our choice to react to change and sometimes even catalyze change to occur. Agile approaches to change allow us to view changes as career catalysts and purposefully take charge of our response. Women leaders whom I've interviewed over the years view themselves as the active producers of their own trajectories rather than victims of circumstance, timing, changes, uncertainty, and luck. Betsy Myers, the former senior adviser on women's issues to Presidents Clinton and Obama, calls for early career women to "own it." Being the driver is about taking ownership of your career direction and your choices. She encourages us all to think: "How do I empower myself instead of feeling like a victim? Take the victim out and put power in."[86] Every time you go through a change, remember Betsy's advice of taking control of your direction and choices—rather than feeling like a victim of circumstances.

Instead of focusing on resistance, focus on response. You can funnel energy into resisting change, or you can use that same time and energy to be intentional about your response to change. Change can be a time of anticipation and excitement. See your reaction to change as a choice that only you can make. It's up to you to choose wisely. An agile approach to change means that we focus on response, and our responses are fluid and flexible based on the changes we're facing and the context we're in. Ask yourself: What can I learn or gain from this change? How can I respond in order to maximize growth and have a positive impact on myself and others? Even when I feel helpless and overwhelmed, I have a choice in my response to situations. What's my end goal here, and how can my responses lead me to a better outcome? You have a choice: Are you choosing resistance, or are you choosing a strategic response?

Focus on the intersection of what matters and what you can influence. The woman whose story I shared at the beginning of this chapter was struggling with the perfect storm of changes and all the associated tensions, office politics, competing priorities, email exchanges, and draining discussions it produced. In times of change and tension, it's essential to ruthlessly prioritize and choose wisely where you invest your time and energy. By taking a step back and identifying this intersection, my client was able to differentiate herself during a time of change by leading her team and still executing to results. Women I've worked with emphasized that their lives include a lot of "noise"—full email inboxes, office politics, requests. "Ignore the noise" is a common refrain. Kristen Robinson of Fidelity offers a helpful mental model about how to sift through incoming distractions. "I focus on the intersection of what matters and what I can control. If it matters and I can control it, I will be relentless. If it does matter but I do not control it, I let it go—not necessarily forever, but for now."[87] Ritva Sotamaa, chief legal officer at Unilever, agrees. "Make sure you focus on the things you can actually influence. I have the ability to let go of the negative issues that do not really matter in the end. I remain optimistic and focus on productivity, rather than getting immersed in unimportant details."[88] As you manage change, stay focused on what matters to you, your team, and your stakeholders and what you can influence. In pressurized times of change, time and energy are not infinite, and you have the choice of where you invest it (think back to chapter 6, on using curiosity to optimize your time investment). Cut through the noise and prioritize strategically.

Choose to be a solution seeker rather than a problem identifier. During times of intense change, it's easy to hyperfocus on what's going wrong instead of focusing on what we can do about it. Whether it's been in my capacity as a career adviser or during my time facilitating programs, I've seen women feel overwhelmed by uncertainty and change, and the associated challenges that come their way. As Marie Forleo, one of Oprah's named thought leaders for the next generation, states: "Everything is figureoutable."[89] I would encourage women throughout their careers to remember that you don't need to have all the answers, but you can use your curious mindset to have the right questions, your courageous mindset to take action, and your agile mindset to think about solutions to try. In other words, you have the power to figure it out by leveraging the mindsets shared in this book. Take the example of the client I've described in this chapter. Helping her company manage the merger and acquisition change was proving difficult, especially since she felt that people were falling into the trap of focusing on problems and complaining about them in a hopeless and helpless manner rather than focusing on potential solutions and ways forward. The negative climate was taking its toll on her emotionally; from a performance standpoint, she felt unable to lead positively in the midst of such negativity. Together we worked on a strategy for her to interrupt unhelpful patterns on calls and in meetings. Whenever challenges or problems were raised, she asked the group critical questions around solutions and best ways to move forward or do things differently. She encouraged her team members to go beyond complaining and to each be someone who comes in with a can-do attitude to solve problems. Whether she was generating solutions to team integration challenges, or new systems or change management obstacles, or the structure of calls, or communication norms and behaviors, or team dynamics and ways of working, she was able to successfully move conversations forward during times of tension and uncertainty. She positioned herself as an agent of change, rather than an obstacle to change, and as a problem-solver. In the end, she was asked to take on a more global role with expanded responsibilities and was rewarded with a raise in compensation package. During a time of overwhelming change, she came to the table with the right mindsets to find solutions rather than complain about problems, and was elevated in her organization because of it.

Take Control of the Sails

There is no denying that experiencing change can be hard. Most sailors don't love the unexpected in their path or course of navigation. Stormy weather, rough seas, tide cycles, and heavy fog can all unexpectedly occur. However, while sailors recognize that they can't control the seas and weather, what they can control is their response to changes. Facing unexpected obstacles in your career and feeling so overwhelmed that you don't take action is the same as a sailor facing a storm and deciding to take down the sails, move away from the ship's wheel, retreat to the cabin below deck, and let fate run its course. Would this be an advisable course of action? By cultivating your agile mindset, you can adopt an agile approach to change, so change isn't something that just happens to you; instead, it puts you in a position of power and choice. The skilled sailor isn't focusing on resistance to unexpected changes; she is focusing on her response.

Aspiration-to-Action

- Describe a change that was initially daunting and overwhelming for you. How did you manage it?
- Describe a change that you managed well. How did you manage it?
- Knowing what you know now, what would you do in the future?
- Write down distinct action steps for improving your approach to change.

Women are empowered through choice. Think about a change on the horizon, one that may or may not happen, an uncertainty you are facing. Capture the choices you have:

- Will I choose being the victim or owning the power of my choice? How will I put this into action?
- Will I choose to focus on my response or on resistance? How will I take action?
- Will I focus on what I can't control or focus on the intersection of what matters and what I can influence? How will I take action?
- Will I focus on identifying problems or on finding solutions? How will I take action?

Risk-Reward-Refine-Repeat

To close out this book, the call to action is to create a Risk-Reward-Refine-Repeat ritual.

By creating a ritual, we can begin to celebrate risk, and outcomes, whether good or bad, and realize that at times, our failures are essential for growth and fulfillment. Where in your life could you create a Risk-Reward-Refine-Repeat ritual? In your teams? In your organization? In a women's group? Describe how you plan to create this ritual and how often your group members will connect and share their risks and rewards.

We have the opportunity to create a ripple effect for other women. Let's cultivate risk and create an enduring impact on our careers and the careers of those around us.

Complete the sentence: *The Risk-Reward-Refine-Repeat ritual I am going to create is...*

....

Launch Your Brilliant Career

WHAT IF INSTEAD OF ASKING "WHY?" you started asking "Why not?" What if you replaced "Why me?" with "Why not me?" What if you swapped quests for perfection with quests for endless possibility and exploration? What if instead of saying "What's the worst that could happen?" and analyzing every worst-case scenario, you started thinking "What's the best that can happen?" What if you started having faith in your capabilities to figure things out in life, regardless of the outcomes of the decisions you take or external variables and obstacles?

What if you started taking a chance on yourself?

Imagine where you could go, what you could accomplish, and who you could become. This book is about moving through fear, embracing uncertainty, making smart moves, optimizing outcomes, and learning how to take those informed chances on yourself. It's about equipping you to step into your best self and career through risk. It's about bridging the gap between your aspirations and actions so that you can craft your most brilliant career.

The career you crave is just beyond your comfort zone. As one executive shared with a group of early career women in Toronto: "You have to get comfortable with being uncomfortable." Moving through discomfort and taking risks requires a curious mindset. You don't need to have all the right answers: You can use the power of questions to form connections, wield influence, and address conflict. It requires focusing on courage over confidence and understanding the aggregate impact of small courageous acts and the power of courageous advocacy, for you and for others. It requires a recognition that life, work, and the world around us are ever-changing, and we have a choice of whether we fight these changes or become fluid, flexible, and agile enough to experiment, embrace uncertainty, and evolve.

As one woman in her twenties shared with me: "You have to play the long game." Once you start working, you realize that college and grad school are short defined periods of time. "Suddenly, you are in this forty-to-fifty-plus-year career, and the time scale changes, and how you think about yourself on that time scale changes," she said. "I realized that my learnings were no longer defined on a quarterly or semester basis. This is a lifelong journey."

Here I want to revisit Nim, whom you met at the beginning of our *Begin Boldly* journey. Nim and I hosted our coaching sessions at her home by the sea. Her space was infused with items that represented her spirit: countless books to feed her voracious love of learning and her curiosity and colorful post-it notes with reminders and mantras to encourage her to "go for it" or to tell her "you have what it takes," her reminders to be courageous. Physical evidence of her agility was everywhere: name tags with her different roles, a map including locations she lived across the world, photos of her running inaugural programs she designed and experimented with, and mementos from her adventures. Nim had piles and piles of notebooks where she captured insights from others, thoughts, new ideas, and reflections. In one notebook she wrote: "because this experiment is as much about my journey as it is about the destination."

Like Nim, remember that your career is an endless experiment and lifelong journey. Risking, reaping rewards, refining approaches, and repeating doesn't have an end point. It's an enduring ritual for all times and all career stages.

Think back to the metaphor at the beginning of this book: Your career is an investment portfolio that you alone can manage and own. Do you want a portfolio that lies stagnant or one that's diversified and dynamic, fueled by your ongoing approach to seeking smart risks, taking many bets, and ultimately, investing in your best future? The earlier you start risking, the more time you will have to experience compounding returns. Yes, you will reap more returns if you start investing in your twenties, but if you are beyond this stage, the second best time to start investing is today—since if you wait until next year, you'll have even less of a runway for risking, reaping rewards, refining approaches, and repeating. The time to start taking risks is now. Take bold moves strategically to bridge the gap between your aspirations and your actions, to build your diversified career portfolio, and reap the rewards of risk. Remember this:

Brilliant careers are seldom built without bold moves.
It is time to live boldly.

Begin Boldly Discussion Guide

The structure of *Begin Boldly* was designed with action in mind. The Put It into Practice, Aspiration-to-Action, and Risk-Reward-Refine-Repeat sections of each chapter can serve as your road map to risking within your own career. The questions below are for broader reflection and discussion after completing the book and the associated exercises. These would be best explored with others who have read the book.

For Women Readers

- Prior to embarking on the *Begin Boldly* journey, how did you define risks? What emotions did the word *risk* elicit?
- Upon completion of this book, how do you define risks now? What emotions does the opportunity to risk elicit? How did your views shift?
- Reflecting on the Risk-Reward-Refine-Repeat sections of this book, what risks can you commit to taking in the next three or six months?
- What do you foresee as the largest obstacles to risk-taking? How do you plan to overcome them?
- We all have the power to create a ripple effect. How are you going to pay it forward and help others to take more risks? How can you contribute to building cultures that celebrate risk in your teams, organizations, institutions, and communities?
- On the flip side, what help and support do you need to implement the Risk-Reward-Refine-Repeat ritual in your own life? Whom can you seek that support from?

On a piece of paper, write yourself a *Begin Boldly* letter that you will open a year from now: Put a reminder in your calendar or ask your *Begin Boldly* accountability advocate or a coach or mentor to keep it safe for you. As you reflect on the key insights in the book, consider these questions:

- What are the key lessons you want to remember?
- How will you embody / be a living example of the *Begin Boldly* lessons and mindsets (curiosity, courage, and agility)?
- In what areas of your life and in what ways will you take more risks?
- What has inspired you the most?
- What new insights do you have about yourself?
- How have your perspectives changed since completing the book?
- What are the areas that you hope to have made progress on a year from now?
- What are the commitments you want to make to yourself?
- How do you now view the world, your career, and your role in it?
- What is your vision / are your hopes for your life after the book?
- How do you hope to use this book on your own and with others in the future?

After completing your letter, discuss your answers to all or some of these questions with a partner or your group. Seal your letter and save it.

For Managers, Educators, Coaches, Mentors, and Sponsors of Early Career Women

Out of the Challenges presented in the book (see below for summary), which Challenges do you believe affect the women you know the most?

Chapter 3: Risking doesn't come without roadblocks, and these detours can easily set women off the course of risk. These include "aspirational collapse," when we give up too readily due to the fact that our initial outcomes don't align with our original aspirations, self-doubt, and the inner critic taking hold.

Chapter 4: Many early career women report that they shy away from one of the most essential career-building activities, networking, due to anxiety and fears. Doing so becomes career limiting, especially at later stages in their careers.

Chapter 5: Women tend to enter challenging conversations and negotiations armed with defensive tools, which are likely to backfire, especially due to societal gender constructs and expectations.

Chapter 6: Women struggle to take risks due to competing priorities and feelings of conflict.

Chapter 7: Until they feel confident, women have a tendency to avoid pursuing stretch goals and opportunities.

Chapter 8: Contrary to popular belief, the workplace is not a meritocracy. Talent and hard work alone will not get women ahead.

Chapter 9: Affinity bias (gravitating toward others like us) can negatively affect women in the workplace, particularly women who are underrepresented in their organization and teams. Affinity bias can affect all women, but because of the existing demographic makeup of most workplaces, it often disproportionately affects women of color.

Chapter 10: Making a big change can be daunting and overwhelming, whether it's in relation to a career or a proposed change in an organization. Such feelings can often lead to inaction, which can have long-term implications for women's careers.

Chapter 11: Women can fall victim to defining themselves in limiting and fixed terms, which in turn holds them back from realizing the bold careers of which they are capable.

Chapter 12: Women, particularly in the earlier stages of their careers, often underestimate their ability to manage change.

As you reflect on these key challenges, think about:

- Which key lessons, concepts, solutions, tools, and techniques from this book can you share with women (e.g., those you coach, mentor, or advise) in your organization to address these challenges? It may be helpful to refer to the relevant chapters related to the Challenges outlined above.
- What exercises can you work through with early career women to ensure that they take action on these insights and solutions to address their challenges? Refer to the Aspiration-to-Action and Risk-Reward-Refine-Repeat sections of chapters 3–12 for ideas.
- What risks can you support women in taking over the next six months? Remember it's up to the risk-taker to define the risk they themselves want to take, but your advocacy and support can be invaluable in spurring ideas and helping those you coach or mentor reimagine risks, assess risks, prepare for risks and outcomes, and make the leap.
- How can you contribute to building cultures that celebrate risk in your teams, organizations, institutions, and communities?

For Organizational Leaders and Executives

This book lays out gender-specific challenges that women face in the workplace. There is a critical role for organizations to play in creating systems, policies, programs, and cultures that interrupt the unhelpful biases, norms, and practices that hold women back. Based on the insights shared in this book, what steps can you take to create a more inclusive organization where women can build brilliant careers?

A refresher on a few select challenges you could discuss:

Affinity bias (gravitating toward those we related to). This can affect who is heard in meetings, who is hired, who is promoted, who gets actionable feedback versus vague feedback, who gets high-value assignments and roles.

The double bind. It's difficult for women to be viewed as competent and likable; men don't face this same complexity.

Conflict and tension. Feelings of conflict between work and priorities outside work are common.

Networking. This includes the lack of access to critical connections.

Negotiation. This includes backlash due to gender constructs for making asks.

Self-demotion. Women's tendencies to underestimate and understate their capabilities and skills can affect hiring, performance reviews, and advancement.

Risk resistance. Lack of safe spaces to take risks, experiment, and grow is an obstacle.

What action steps can you take to address these challenges at an organizational level?

Most of the executives I work with have great intent, but their outcomes don't match their intentions. Ask yourself: Do my outcomes match my intentions? For instance, if your intention is to create a vibrant and inclusive organization but you lack female representation in leadership roles, there's a gap.

If you answered no, how will you close the gap between your inclusion intentions and your inclusion outcomes? What outcomes will you measure?

How can you contribute to building cultures that celebrate risk in your teams, organizations, institutions, and communities? Taking action with these ideas, tools, and resources will help to build more inclusive and vibrant organizations and communities where women can live and lead boldly.

Notes

1 Orit Gadiesh and Julie Coffman, "Companies Drain Women's Ambition after Only Two Years," *Harvard Business Review*, May 18, 2015, https://hbr.org/2015/05/companies-drain-womens-ambition-after-only-2-years.

2 Robin J. Ely, Pamela Stone, and Colleen Ammerman, "Rethink What You Know about High Achieving Women," *Harvard Business Review*, December 2014, https://hbr.org/2014/12/rethink-what-you-know-about-high-achieving-women.

3 Jess Huang et al., "Women in the Workplace 2019," Mckinsey and Company and Lean In, 2019, https://womenintheworkplace.com/2019.

4 Christianne Corbett and Catherine Hill, "Graduating to a Pay Gap: The Earnings of Women and Men One Year after College Graduation," American Association of University Women, 2012, https://ww3.aauw.org/files/2013/02/graduating-to-a-pay-gap-the-earnings-of-women-and-men-one-year-after-college-graduation.pdf; Christie Silva and Nancy Carter, "Women Don't Go After the Big Jobs with Gusto: True or False?," *Harvard Business Review*, October 13, 2011, https://hbr.org/2011/10/women-dont-go-after-the-big-jo.

5 Huang et al., "Women in the Workplace 2019."

6 Rachel Thomas et al., "Women in the Workplace 2020," Mckinsey and Company and Lean In, 2020, https://womenintheworkplace.com/2020.

7 Ibid.

8 Maria Konnikova, "Lean Out: The Dangers for Women Who Negotiate," *New Yorker*, June 10, 2014, https://www.newyorker.com/science/maria-konnikova/lean-out-the-dangers-for-women-who-negotiate.

9 Lauren Noël and Christie Hunter Arscott, "Make It Happen: How Women Leaders Can Unleash Their Strengths," QUEST: A Global Leadership Institute for Early Career Women, 2018, https://herquest.org/research/documents/18_QUEST_Make%20It%20Happen%20Research.pdf.

10 KPMG, "2019 KPMG Women's Leadership Study: Risk, Resilience, Reward," 2019, https://info.kpmg.us/content/dam/info/en/news-perspectives/pdf/2019/KPMG_Womens_Leadership_Study.pdf.

11 Noël and Hunter Arscott, "Make It Happen."

12 Doug Sundheim, "Do Women Take as Many Risks as Men?," *Harvard Business Review*, February 27, 2013, https://hbr.org/2013/02/do-women-take-as-many-risks-as.

13 Noël and Hunter Arscott, "Make It Happen."

14 Danielle Pacquette, "Your Lifetime Earnings Are Probably Decided in Your Twenties," *Washington Post,* February 10, 2015, https://www.washingtonpost.com/news/wonk/wp/2015/02/10/your-lifetime-earnings-are-probably-determined-in-your-twenties/.

15 Carol S. Dweck, *Mindset: The New Psychology of Success*, updated ed. (New York: Ballantine Books, 2007).

16 Noël and Hunter Arscott, "Make It Happen."

17 Ibid.

18 Daniel Kahneman, *Thinking, Fast and Slow* (New York: Farrar, Straus and Giroux, 2013).

19 Liz Fosslien and Mollie West Duffy, @LizandMollie, Twitter, July 7, 2021, https://twitter.com/lizandmollie/status/1412608553773305857.

20 Noël and Hunter Arscott, "Make It Happen."

21 Ibid.

22 Sundheim, "Do Women Take as Many Risks as Men?"

23 Katty Kay and Claire Shipman, "The Confidence Gap," *Atlantic*, 2014, https://www.theatlantic.com/magazine/archive/2014/05/the-confidence-gap/359815/.

24 Noël and Hunter Arscott, "Make It Happen."

25 Silva and Carter, "Women Don't Go After the Big Jobs."

26 Alison Wood Brooks and Leslie K. John, "The Surprising Power of Questions," *Harvard Business Review*, 2018, https://hbr.org/2018/05/the-surprising-power-of-questions.

27 Julia Hanna, "Leveraging Female Talent: Star Women and the Ways Companies Keep Them," Harvard Business School Alumni Stories Online, March 1, 2013, https://www.alumni.hbs.edu/stories/Pages/story-bulletin.aspx?num=1160.

28 Noël and Hunter Arscott, "Make It Happen."

29 Tiziana Casciaro et al., "The Contaminating Effects of Building Instrumental Ties: How Networking Can Make Us Feel Dirty," *Sage Journal*, 2014, https://journals.sagepub.com/doi/abs/10.1177/0001839214554990?journalCode=asqa&.

30 Sheila Brassel, Joy Ohm, and Dnika J. Travis, "Curiosity Powers Allyship to Create Change," Catalyst, 2021, https://www.catalyst.org/reports/allyship-curiosity-employees-of-color/.

31 Michael Kardis, Amit Kumar, and Nicholas Epley, "Overly Shallow: Miscalibrated Expectations Create a Barrier to Deeper Conversations," *American Psychological Association*, 2021 https://psycnet.apa.org/record/2021-88608-001.

32 Ibid.

33 Nicholas Epley, Michael Kardas, and Amit Kumar, "Small Talk Is Boring. Our Research Shows How You Can Do It Better," *Washington Post*, 2021, https://www.washingtonpost.com/outlook/2021/10/13/posteverything-small-talk-deeper-conversations.

34 Jamie Harrison, "Battle of the Sexes: Are Women More Self-Conscious in the Office Than Men?," *Black Enterprise*, February 19, 2013, https://www.blackenterprise.com/study-workplace-perception-office-women-care-more/.

35 Karen Huag et al., "It Doesn't Hurt to Ask: Question-Asking Increases Liking," *American Psychology Association*, 2017, https://psycnet.apa.org/record/2017–18566–001.

36 Erica Boothby et al., "The Liking Gap in Conversations: Do People Like Us More Than We Think?," *Sage Journals*, 2018, https://journals.sagepub.com/doi/abs/10.1177/0956797618783714

37 Noël and Hunter Arscott, "Make It Happen."

38 Lauren Noël and Christie Hunter Arscott, "BlackRock's Story," QUEST: A Global Leadership Institute for Early Career Women, 2015, https://her-quest.org/research/documents/15_blackroot.pdf.

39 Elizabeth Agnvall, *Women and Negotiation*, SHRM, December 1, 2007, https://www.shrm.org/hr-today/news/hr-magazine/pages/1207agenda_careerdev.aspx.

40 Konnikova, "Lean Out."

41 Adam Grant, "The Power of Powerless Communication," TEDx Talks, YouTube video, May 23, 2013, The power of powerless communication: Adam Grant at TEDxEast.

42 "The Perils of Powerful Speech," Program on Negotiation, Harvard Law School, Daily Blog, July 25, 2012, https://www.pon.harvard.edu/daily/business-negotiations/the-perils-of-powerful-speech/.

43 Katie Liljenquist and Adam D. Galinsky, "Win Over an Opponent by Asking for Advice," *Harvard Business Review*, June 17, 2014, https://hbr.org/2014/06/win-over-an-opponent-by-asking-for-advice.

44 "Five Ways to Negotiate Like a Pro," *Y Magazine*, Brigham Young University, Winter 2014, https://magazine.byu.edu/article/5-ways-to-negotiate-like-a-pro/.

45 Noël and Hunter Arscott, "BlackRock's Story."

46 Ibid.

47 Jack Kelly, "Indeed Study Shows That Worker Burnout Is at Frighteningly High Levels: Here Is What You Need to Do Now," *Forbes*, April 5, 2021, https://www.forbes.com/sites/jackkelly/2021/04/05/indeed-study-shows-that-worker-burnout-is-at-frighteningly-high-levels-here-is-what-you-need-to-do-now/.

48 Rachel King, "What's Fueling 'The Great Resignation' among Younger Generations?," *Fortune*, August 26, 2021, https://fortune.com/2021/08/26/pandemic-burnout-career-changes-great-resignation-adobe/.

49 Betsy Myers and John D. Mann, *Take the Lead: Motivate, Inspire, and Bring Out the Best in Yourself and Everyone around You* (Atria Books, 2012).

50 Stewart D. Friedman, *Total Leadership: Be a Better Leader, Have a Richer Life* (Harvard Business Press, 2008).

51 Joyce Ehrlinger and David Dunning, "How Chronic Self-Views Influence (and Potentially Mislead) Estimates of Performance," *Journal of Personality and Social Psychology* 84 (2003): 5–17, https://doi.org/10.1037/0022-3514.84.1.5.

52 Tara Sophia Mohr, "Why Women Don't Apply for Jobs Unless They Are 100% Qualified," *Harvard Business Review*, August 25, 2014, https://hbr.org/2014/08/why-women-dont-apply-for-jobs-unless-theyre-100-qualified.

53 Kay and Shipman, "Confidence Gap."

54 Christine Exley and Judd Kessler, "The Gender Gap in Self-Promotion," National Bureau of Economic Research, October 2019, revised May 2021, https://www.nber.org/system/files/working_papers/w26345/w26345.pdf.

55 Noël and Hunter Arscott, "Make It Happen."

56 Ibid.

57 Ibid.

58 Lois P. Frankel, *Nice Girls Don't Get the Corner Office: Unconscious Mistakes Women Make That Sabotage Their Careers* (Grand Central Publishing, 2014).

59 Nancy M. Carter and Christine Silva, *The Myth of the Ideal Worker: Does Doing All the Right Things Really Get Women Ahead?* (Catalyst, 2011), https://www.catalyst.org/wp-content/uploads/2019/02/The_Myth_of_the_Ideal_Worker_Does_Doing_All_the_Right_Things_Really_Get_Women_Ahead.pdf.

60 Noël and Hunter Arscott, "Make It Happen."

61 Rhea E. Steinpreis et al., "The Impact of Gender on the Review of the Curricula Vitae of Job Applicants and Tenure Candidates: A National Empirical Study," *Sex Roles* 41, nos. 7–8 (1999): 509–28.

62 Eric L. Uhlmann and Geoffrey L. Cohen, "Constructed Criteria: Redefining Merit to Justify Discrimination," *Psychological Science* 16 (2005): 474–80.

63 Rebekah Bastian, "Personality-Based Performance Reviews Are Fine to Give Women—As Long As Men Get Them Too," *Forbes*, March 8, 2019, https://www.forbes.com/sites/rebekahbastian/2019/03/08/personality-based-performance-reviews-are-fine-to-give-women-as-long-as-men-get-them-too/?sh=2626281c1667.

64 Mark Peters, "The Hidden Sexism in Workplace Language," BBC, March 30, 2017, https://www.bbc.com/worklife/article/20170329-the-hidden-sexism-in-workplace-language.

65 Ibid.

66 Noël and Hunter Arscott, "Make It Happen."

67 Lauren Noël and Christie Hunter Arscott, "What Executives Need to Know about Early Career Women," QUEST: Global Leadership Institute for Early Career Women, 2015.

68 Lean In, "What Is Affinity Bias," *Fifty Ways to Fight Bias*, https://leanin.org/education/what-is-affinity-bias.

69 Pooja Jain-Link and Julia Taylor Kennedy, "The Sponsor Dividend," Coqual (formerly CTI), 2019, https://coqual.org/wp-content/uploads/2020/09/CoqualTheSponsorDividend_KeyFindingsCombined090720.pdf.

70 Emily Crockett, "The Amazing Tool That Women in the White House Use to Fight Gender Bias," Vox, September 14, 2016, https://www.vox.com/2016/9/14/12914370/white-house-obama-women-gender-bias-amplification.

71 Noël and Hunter Arscott, "Make It Happen."

72 Noël and Hunter Arscott, "What Executives Need to Know about Early Career Women."

73 Noël and Hunter Arscott, "Make It Happen."

74 Jack Zenger and Joseph Folkman, "How Age and Gender Affect Self-Improvement," *Harvard Business Review*, January 5, 2016, https://hbr.org/2016/01/how-age-and-gender-affect-self-improvement?curator=MediaREDEF.

75 Herminia Ibarra, *Working Identity: Unconventional Strategies for Reinventing Your Career* (Harvard Business School Press, 2004).

76 Noël and Hunter Arscott, "Make It Happen."

77 Ibid.

78 James Clear, *Atomic Habits: An Easy and Proven Way to Build Good Habits and Break Bad Ones* (Penguin Publishing Group, 2018).

79 Zenger and Folkman, "How Age and Gender Affect Self-Improvement."

80 Noël and Hunter Arscott, "Make It Happen."

81 Elizabeth Gilbert, *Big Magic: Creative Living beyond Fear* (Penguin Publishing Group, 2016).

82 Noël and Hunter Arscott, "Make It Happen."

83 Gilbert, *Big Magic*.

84 Noël and Hunter Arscott, "Make It Happen."

85 Ibid.

86 Ibid.

87 Ibid.

88 Ibid.

89 Marie Forleo, *Everything Is Figureoutable* (Penguin Publishing Group, 2019).

Acknowledgments

My father once told me, "Life is a team sport," and I now know that writing a book is no different. This book wouldn't have been possible without an incredible team.

First, thank you to the team at Berrett-Koehler (BK). Writing this book has felt like putting an overwhelming puzzle together, piece by piece, and hoping that all the pieces fit (and that I didn't lose any pieces in the process). I am so glad to have partnered with a publisher so skilled at complex puzzles! Thank you for taking a chance on a first-time author with bold ideas and aspirations for a book to support early career women. While there are too many critical team players to name, I want to thank the first-draft editors and copyeditor, BK leadership, and everyone involved in art direction, design, production, marketing, sales, and more. Thank you to the Penguin Random House team for partnering with BK to distribute this work.

To my editor, Anna Leinberger: Your editorial acumen, wordcraft, thematic prowess, critical eye, and gender-intelligent lens made this book what it is. Thank you for pushing me and reminding me throughout the process what risk-taking is all about.

To Betsy Myers: I feel so fortunate to know the woman behind the impressive bio. Having a window into her intellect and soul has been nothing but an honor. Your authenticity, infectious energy, and compelling candor come through in all that you do. You are a breath of fresh air in a world that needs more vulnerability, transparency, and honest conversation about what it takes to build a brilliant career and life.

To Alicia Simons: You've been with me from day one, when this book was just an aspiration. Thank you for your long-term dedication and for being one of the driving forces that helped me translate that aspiration into action. Your advocacy is a living example of what women need in order to take risks on themselves. Thank you for being in my corner!

To Elizabeth Doughty: Thank you for your critical eye and for helping translate the ideas in my head into ideas on a page.

To my research partner Lauren Noël: Our shared passion and research interests helped form the foundation for this work. I am grateful for our connection. To Chantal: Thank you for your selfless support and insightful collaboration. To Doug and Joanne: Thank you for the platform to do this important work.

To my parents: Thank you for your unconditional love, understanding, and remarkable tolerance as I've navigated the ebbs and flows of writing this book and riding the ever-changing waves of my career and life. You are not only my pillars of support but also my retaining wall in the storms.

To my husband: Your support of my career and professional pursuits knows no bounds. Thank you for your unwavering belief in me and my ability to positively influence the lives of others.

To my son: Mummy finally finished her book. Time for more adventures.

To my extended family—including my sister Risa and friends—you know who you are! Thank you for understanding my absence and exhaustion and supporting my journey and long-standing commitment to the gender field.

To Nim: You are my fearless cheerleader, as well as a curious critical thinker, courageous champion, and confidant. Thank you for bringing light, energy, and enthusiasm into the most onerous of my book-writing days. Thank you for your bright spark, your inspiration, your enduring energy, your accountability, our intellectual sparring, and our soul connection.

To the amazing women I've researched and worked with throughout the years: You continue to infuse my career with meaning and momentum, and I am forever grateful for your contributions.

Finally, I'd like to thank the researchers, advocates, and activists whose work continues to inspire me and whose tireless dedication to the field of gender and women's studies has laid the foundation for my work in this space.

I stand on the sacrifices of a million women before me thinking what can I do to make this mountain taller so the women after me can see farther. —Rupi Kaur

Index

for, *97–98, 100, 101*; gender
disparities in, 4, 84–85;
risk-reward-refine-repeat
exercises, 90–91, 107–8, 118–19;
small acts of courage, 83–91;
solutions, 85–87, 94–99,
112–13. *See also* advocacy;
self-advocacy
cover letters, 100, 105
COVID-19 pandemic, effects of, 4,
74, 103, 121
critical thinking skills, 67
culture "fit," 111, 113–14
curious mindset, 2, 36, 37, 43–82;
in agile experimentation,
129; aspiration-to-action
exercises, 55–56, 71, 78–79;
bold MOVES method, 56,
71, 79; challenges, 46–47,
59–61, 74; for connectivity,
45–57; framework for, 65,
66; for influence, 58–72, 126;
for optimizing investments,
73–79; risk-reward-refine-
repeat exercises, 56–57, 71–72,
79; solutions, 47–48, 61–65,
74–76. *See also* negotiating;
networking; questioning

debating, 59, 60
"deep talk," 52–53, 56
defensiveness, 59
Deloitte Consulting, 60
De Swardt, Nim, 1–3, 26, 44, 63–64,
124, 152
discussion guide, 155–59
distractions, 147–48
diversity and inclusion initiatives,
129, 132
double bind: and courageous
advocacy, 94, 115; using
curiosity to overcome, 53–54,
62, 68, 69, 70
doubt. *See* self-doubt
Dweck, Carol S., 19, 136, 137

early career years: advice needed
for, 9–10; experimentation
during, 124, 127; gender
disparities in, 3–5, 93, 137;
momentum building, xiii, 18,
37, 47, 103; risk-taking crucial
during, xii-xiii, 152; "the early
career progress principle," 124;
uncertainty of, xi
education, 14, 40, 47–48
elevator pitch, 95, 98
empathy, 56, 64
end-game plan, *26, 30–31, 34, 41,*
56, 71. *See also* aspiration-to-
action; goals
entry-level jobs, 4, 18
Esquel Group, 146
Everday Massive, 2
expectations, clarifying, 50–51,
76–77, 78, 79
experimentation, 122–35; cycle of,
128; defining, 132–33; evolving,
130–31; framework for, 128–34;
vs. overanalyzing, 123–24;
as a risk-taking trait, 2, 152;
with small scale trials, 124–27,
131–32

failure: backup plans for, 30–31;
fear of, 12, 136, 137; gender
disparities in penalizing, 33;
gender disparities in viewing,
19–20; as a reward, 12–13, 17–18
Federal Reserve Bank of Boston,
140
Federal Reserve Bank of New York,
18, 140
feedback: learning from, 17;
providing, 110, 111, 113, 118
Fidelity, 138, 147
flexibility. *See* agile mindset
focus, 147–49
follow-up questions, 51, 52, 54, 61,
65
Forleo, Marie, 148

About the Author

Christie Hunter Arscott is an internationally recognized advisor, author, and speaker dedicated to creating more vibrant, dynamic, and equitable career paths and organizations.

As one of the first Rhodes Scholars to pursue graduate research in women's studies, Christie has been named by *Thinkers50* as "one of the top management thinkers likely to shape the future of how organizations are managed and led."

Christie currently serves on the Women's Leadership Board of the Women and Public Policy Program at Harvard Kennedy School. Her research and writing have been included across international publications, including in the Thinkers50 book: *Dear CEO: 50 Personal Letters from the World's Leading Business Thinkers*, and *Harvard Business Review*'s collection of the top *HBR* articles on diversity.

Christie has spoken at the World Economic Forum, Harvard Business School, the University of Oxford's Saïd Business School, and the Global Women's Forum for the Economy and Society, among many other leading organizations, conferences, and institutions across the globe.

Christie holds a bachelor's degree in political science from Brown University, a certificate of distinction in general management from Stanford University's Graduate School of Business, and two master's degrees with a focus on gender research from the University of Oxford. She formerly served as a consultant and diversity and inclusion subject matter expert within Deloitte's U.S. consulting practice.

For media, press, speaking, or services inquiries, Christie can be reached through her website: **ChristieHunterArscott.com**.

Berrett–Koehler
Publishers

Berrett-Koehler is an independent publisher dedicated to an ambitious mission: *Connecting people and ideas to create a world that works for all.*

Our publications span many formats, including print, digital, audio, and video. We also offer online resources, training, and gatherings. And we will continue expanding our products and services to advance our mission.

We believe that the solutions to the world's problems will come from all of us, working at all levels: in our society, in our organizations, and in our own lives. Our publications and resources offer pathways to creating a more just, equitable, and sustainable society. They help people make their organizations more humane, democratic, diverse, and effective (and we don't think there's any contradiction there). And they guide people in creating positive change in their own lives and aligning their personal practices with their aspirations for a better world.

And we strive to practice what we preach through what we call "The BK Way." At the core of this approach is *stewardship,* a deep sense of responsibility to administer the company for the benefit of all of our stakeholder groups, including authors, customers, employees, investors, service providers, sales partners, and the communities and environment around us. Everything we do is built around stewardship and our other core values of *quality, partnership, inclusion, and sustainability.*

This is why Berrett-Koehler is the first book publishing company to be both a B Corporation (a rigorous certification) and a benefit corporation (a for-profit legal status), which together require us to adhere to the highest standards for corporate, social, and environmental performance. And it is why we have instituted many pioneering practices (which you can learn about at www.bkconnection.com), including the Berrett-Koehler Constitution, the Bill of Rights and Responsibilities for BK Authors, and our unique Author Days.

We are grateful to our readers, authors, and other friends who are supporting our mission. We ask you to share with us examples of how BK publications and resources are making a difference in your lives, organizations, and communities at www.bkconnection.com/impact.

Dear reader,

Thank you for picking up this book and welcome to the worldwide BK community! You're joining a special group of people who have come together to create positive change in their lives, organizations, and communities.

What's BK all about?

Our mission is to connect people and ideas to create a world that works for all.

Why? Our communities, organizations, and lives get bogged down by old paradigms of self-interest, exclusion, hierarchy, and privilege. But we believe that can change. That's why we seek the leading experts on these challenges—and share their actionable ideas with you.

A welcome gift

To help you get started, we'd like to offer you a **free copy** of one of our bestselling ebooks:

www.bkconnection.com/welcome

When you claim your **free ebook**, you'll also be subscribed to our blog.

Our freshest insights

Access the best new tools and ideas for leaders at all levels on our blog at ideas.bkconnection.com.

Sincerely,

Your friends at Berrett-Koehler

Certified

Corporation